Towards A Visual Culture

Educating through Television

Towards A Visual Culture

Educating through Television

CALEB GATTEGNO

OUTERBRIDGE & DIENSTFREY

Distributed by E. P. Dutton & Company

Acknowledgments

I wish to take this opportunity to thank my colleagues and friends at Schools for the Future in New York City for their unreserved assistance. In particular, some of the trustees have taken the necessary steps to have each technical statement checked by professionals.

My two secretaries, Mrs. Yolanda Maranga and Mrs. Ann Siebert, who have typed and retyped the several versions of the text without even a murmur, deserve special mention and thanks.

Outerbridge & Dienstfrey
200 West 72nd Street
New York City 10023

Dedicated to
Shakti,
Uma Devi,
and
Ashish Caleb

Table of Contents

Preface

This book on education and on television's role in education has been written to encourage discussion about issues that are becoming more important every-day but are still not being looked at closely enough.

It is a slender text for a huge area. Many questions that could have been asked have been left out, others are scarcely touched upon. Still, it is far from a cursory look at education and television. With regard to education, it is, in terms of the author, a summing up of more than forty years of practice and of thinking, involving face-to-face contact with all sorts of learnings. With regard to television, the proof of the seriousness of the discussion will be found in the leads presented here for programs that could be translated—this is known rather than just believed—into actual and successful shows.

Readers, I believe, will not need long to find that they are confronted with questions that will mobilize their creative mind and will force them into thinking anew about matters to which they now may rarely turn to stimulate their perception of reality, though such matters have been cardinal in the initial stages of everybody's growth. If a public discusson of any of these considerations ensues, the publication now of this book as it is will have been justified.

We need to be a legion of workers to make a success of the place of television in education. But we first need to ask the right questions. Only after the answers emerge can we produce the programs that will satisfy the true needs of growth—and not just in the young but in each of us. To summon the huge competence to meet these demands will in itself be an education for those who will lead in this field.

Technologists foresee developments in television that will put the whole world at the disposal of every home via satellite and, via computers, all the canned knowledge accumulated to date. They no longer see any insurmountable obstacle in creating such equipment. Nor do they believe there will be a problem, via the computer and the telephone, in providing every individual in his own home with immediate access to the programs he believes he needs in order to be informed at once on what matters to him.

Since technologists can easily perform these tasks, we do not need to work on them. What is left to consider is less easy and more debatable, for once we leave the fields of matter and electromagnetism, criteria to guide our steps are less readily available. This book has attempted to provide a gathering of such criteria, so that readers can come to feel less of a discontinuity between the soundness (such as it is) of the hardware and that of the software. These criteria are in fact also capable of integrating the progress of technology into the growth of men's awareness of themselves as living within a universe that has components that now are treated almost solely by men called technologists. The proposals in this book are samples of this synthetic approach, of which education is so much in need. The approach has of course a place every time we are asked to think of complex things in a complex way.

C. Gattegno
New York City, January 1969

Introduction
Educating Televiewers
by Educating Telecasters

Being of age does not guarantee knowledge of oneself.

The two decades of existence of television are no guarantee either that the medium knows itself.

In this book an attempt will be made to reach the reality of television and link it to the reality of education, for in the area of education today, television may have its greatest contribution to make.

Most of what follows in this text about television has been learned directly, i.e. by simply viewing and letting the events affect the viewer with whatever they had to offer a mind that surrendered to them. No reference to any current literature will be found in the following pages because the author wished to distinguish a testimony from a scholarly work. The more competent and erudite readers will easily fill the gap and, when necessary, will attribute to whomever it belongs, the paternity of any idea expressed before this book appeared.

It seems in any case that whatever is of value in this field must have been uncovered by a method comparable to the one used by the writer and that the differences in the discoveries result only from differences in the preparation of the observers prior to their attempt to examine the problems before them.

The writer had been introduced to television late in his life and, at the beginning, only casually. When he came to own a black and white set early in 1966, he began to view the material on it consciously almost every minute he looked at the set. Whatever he noted could have been noted by anyone, since it was there to be perceived. So he did not think his observations were of any special value to other viewers until he was told by people who could have known much more about television than did he (because of their more frequent opportunities to watch it), that they had not seen what he had seen until he made them aware of it.

So he began to consider sharing with as many as would be interested the findings that seemed to be special to him because of a certain watchfulness he had cultivated over the years. This book offers for the first time, in a compact manner, what he knows to be present when he looks at a television set alive with an image that has been placed there by technology and for the reasons that move television's personnel.

Sometime before he became a regular television viewer, the writer had worked on films for education (including films for teachers' education), asking himself what were the characteristics of knowing through sight, distinguishing this way of knowing from other ways of knowing and marveling at its efficacy. He also had studied images and imagery, children's drawings, dreams of all ages, and found in the dynamics of imagery a great source of ideas and new thoughts.*

What struck him particularly in these studies was that his functionings usually went in pairs—taste and smell, speech and hearing—but that sight was alone. While his hearing controlled his speech and his smell

---

Not all of these studies have been reported on in print. Some of the findings can be found in For the Teaching of Mathematics, Vols. 1 and 2 (Educational Explorers, Ltd., Reading, England).

his taste, there was nothing to "tell" his sight, except itself, what he was seeing. In fact, we all know the endless discussions that arise when people pose such problems as: "Do we see the same green?". For another person to know what *you* see, you have to tell him in words into which you put whatever you can of your vision, and he has to interpret your words. There are no means for one person to see what another is seeing.

At least that was what the writer thought until he realized that man, by inventing the cathode ray tube of television, had made himself capable of making people see what he sees and conversely. He realized then that television was much more than an easy way of having for a fee or for nothing (or rather for putting up with commercials) all sorts of spectacles at home. Rather, it was a man-made device that provided each of us with a visual respondent for one's vision.

At once many of the marvelous applications of this gift presented themselves. Since one was capable of visualizing so much in one's own ordinary mental functioning and, prior to television, was able only (as is being done here again!) to verbalize about such visual perceptions, it seemed clear to the writer, who experienced a new sense of freedom as a result, that an extraordinary power had been added to man's existing powers, one that could affect millions at once and in chosen directions.

When he spoke of this new awareness—of television as the companion of man's sight—even to professionals in the field of television, no one responded. It was at first a vision that, like many others, had to find its expression outside words.

In the two years that have passed, the writer has learned a great deal more. All his findings confirmed his original perception and have made it more functional, more adequate, so that he now has at his disposal not a bright idea but a universe with many entries and many technical facilities with which to use the tremendous gift of television for the benefit of all.

This book is the verbal transmutation of what he has learned, a call to use television for what it can give, which is really tremendous and by most still unsuspected.

Sight, even though used by all of us so naturally, has not yet produced its civilization. Sight is swift, comprehensive, simultaneously analytic and synthetic. It requires so little energy to function, as it does, at the speed of light, that it permits our minds to receive and hold an infinite number of items of information in a fraction of a second. With sight, infinities are given at once; wealth is its description. In contrast to the speed of light, we need *time* to talk and to express what we want to say. The inertia of photons is nil compared to the inertia of our muscles and chains of bones.

Man has functioned as a seer and embraced vastnesses for millenia. But only recently, through television, has he been able to shift from the clumsiness of speech (however miraculous and far reaching) as means of expression and therefore of communication, to the powers of the dynamic, infinite visual expression, thus enabling him to share with everybody immense dynamic wholes in no time.

Even if for some time speech will remain the most common way of letting others know what we know, we can foresee the coming of an era where the processing of visual material will be as easy as our comprehension of talk but swifter because of the former's lack of inertia; and through its spatialization by electrons, we shall be able to share vast conscious experiences at once. Today large novels are needed for this.

The future is requiring that we learn to consider ever larger wholes in whatever social position we find ourselves. As the world becomes more easily accessible, and its cultures affect each other more profoundly, and more people become involved in all sorts of functions in one situation, etc., we are finding that the meeting of complex situations is more the rule than the exception. A visual culture obviously is the answer to such a trend (which it did not create).

It is already with us, but our habits of thought, our very use of words make it difficult to notice. When we are shown a picture that has a caption, we run to the caption, understand the words first, and only then look—and only for a second—at the picture. Observing visitors to a museum of art will make this plain to all.

These are some of the considerations that will be examined in Chapter 1.

The awareness that sight is a far swifter means of expression and communication than speech denotes one of the powers of our mind. A number of such powers will be examined in this text because they are relevant to understanding the connection between awareness and education. One of them will permit us to reach the meaning of childhood, whose characteristics we shall study in some detail in the second chapter of this book, where we will consider what it is that people bring with them to the television experience.

By childhood we understand a succession of clearly marked periods of change in each of our lives, up to the period, which we can agree usually lasts for a long stretch of time, where we change less or, at least visibly, not much.

The method we shall use to understand the meaning of childhood will be to ask ourselves, "How do we make sense of any of the states or any of the experiences we find ourselves in?" and then link this problem both to the question, "When have we prepared ourselves for achieving such an awareness?" and to what we can observe of the things that children of different ages do with themselves.

Is it not true that every adult who is not vegetating, is all the time trying to make sense of what his life as a whole is about? Or is trying to make sense of why he cannot see the interests of others as they do? Or they his? To ask such questions as, "What did I do, say, at the age of one, which absorbed all my energies?"—or, "What is left of the experiences of that age in my subsequent years until now?"—is one way of reaching insights that are of paramount importance when we wish to find a true guide in life for any action that seeks to affect people of ages other than our own.

Education is an attempt by some people to offer others (or oneself) the means that will help the process of making sense of one's relation to oneself and the various universes around one. Hence, education is about awareness—and about awareness of one's awareness, for without the latter an individual will not develop his own inner criteria for truth, the measures that give everyone the responsibility for his actions in and upon the universe, particularly the universe of relationships.

That television can play a role in this sort of education is the basic proposal that informs chapters three and four of this text.

Besides the instrument and what viewers bring with them, there is a third factor that must be considered in examining television, and this of course is what appears on the tube. This we shall think of in human terms rather than as a product.

For our purpose what matters most is the fact that people, with all their preconceptions, prejudices, tastes, fears, character and imagination, talents and opportunities, are involved in the various rooms where programs are born and brought to the stage of showing. So long as these people are not properly informed of what is an essential part of their particular activity— the making of television programs—how could we expect that they act otherwise than via their preconceptions and opinions?

Hence if we want to see programs that are true to the possibilities of the instrument and the realities of viewers, we must investigate the extent to which the modes of thought of all those involved in making the programs are compatible and in harmony with what is asked for in the use of television to produce a true education. If it is found that programers are unaware of a basic set of elements that are necessary for the educational success of their programs and unwittingly neglect it, then an education of telecasters must take place before any program has a real chance of being educationally meaningful.

A moment of reflection on the importance the television industry attributes to ratings will show that it is almost always a posteriori that shows are assessed. Those who take into account most of the components that constitute television could also forecast the ratings and slowly teach others how to stop playing at using television as no more than a changing reaction to changing whims and replace such treatment by a mixture of *art* and *science* that knows its targets and reaches them.

It is the contention of this book that in the field of education by television the essential elements of this mixture exist and that it is possible, by creative and intelligent use of them, to score high marks deliberately and consistently, without any need to guess about the tastes of the audience. The "science" part of the mixture is summarized in chapters one and two of this work. References to the "art" that is needed will be found in the specific proposals of Chapter 3. To transform these proposals into programs will require all the techniques, technologies, and knowhow available to all the producers, directors, technicians who will be called in to develop the programs.

All that can be done in a book like this is to show how an understanding of the essential characteristics of viewing and of the capabilities of the instrument can be transmuted into a set of programs that respect all the demands put on a product destined to reach the screen, demands made by the producers and their aides, who together are the most knowledgeable about such matters.

The space of this book will not be devoted to

criticism of educational programs as they are currently
conceived. The book seems better used if every page
is taken up with considerations that push us forward
in the study of what matters for the successful use of
television in education.

In this introduction we can say that the educator
in the writer could not be satisfied in using the elec-
tronic beam simply to produce the image of a speaker,
however good and knowledgeable that speaker might
be. Instead, he has posed for himself the question of
what is educational in the mental dialogue between the
viewer and a beam that reflects the intentions of minds
who can visualize the variousness, wealth, depth, and
treasured repercussions upon others, of the seer in
every mind.

We would ask no more of viewers than that they
look; the rest, i.e. making them *see*, is the joint job of
the programers with their technicians and the television set. If the programs have respected the reality
of seeing, education will happen, an education that
does not need remembering, for a part of oneself will
have been forever mobilized by the complex image on
the tube, available always to be evoked at will or trig-
gered up by association. The visual powers of the
mind will have been fertilized because they have been
called upon to function and to produce meaningful,
dynamic equivalents of the time spent in viewing.

Which means that television provides the first
occasion such a high yield can be contemplated in
education. The first occasion that highly sophisticated
gifts functioning from almost the beginning of life
can be used systematically for the growth of one's insights into endless avenues of experience and experiencing.

For the first time in the history of education, the
equation of time consumed for learning and the
amount of learning accomplished will show that, because of the great speed of light, much more can be
achieved by everyone in every unit of time.

1.

The Medium of Television

From physics we can learn what makes it possible for a set to present a visual image. We can learn how an electron beam, directed toward the surface of a screen on which a luminescent substance has been spread, is made to scan the screen long enough to produce the illusion of a photographic reproduction.

Beyond these facts, there are others that need to be learned if one is to understand from first principles the electromagnetic phenomena involved from the moment a camera is directed towards an object to the appearance of its image on a screen in a home.

All this we shall either assume is known by the readers or, because it is altogether unnecessary to understand what follows, irrelevant and not called for.

The images on the screen are watched by eyes, and one could equally well say that it is necessary to know as much of the phenomena involved in sight as of the phenomena that enable the set to work. This too we shall either assume to be known to the readers or irrelevant.

1. When we talk of the medium of television we are clearly concerned with what people see on the screen,

how they see it, the way it affects them physiologically, psychologically, socially, and spiritually. Even the study of physics is a human study. Hence, here we shall only consider the human meanings of the medium of television, leaving to other writers the aspects mentioned above.

2.   Though viewing is no doubt a very personal act, we shall write about it here in general terms, thus neglecting individual differences and stressing what is common.

Eyes, looking at television (as at everything else) will perceive colors, shades, and hues if these are present, even though it is impossible to determine the exact variations perceived by each of the viewers. In fact, words to describe such matters are conveniently vague, so that to answer yes to the question, "Is his nose red?" does not require that the questioner and the answerer see the "same" red but simply that they both acknowledge that the word red, so far as their experience has given it meaning, is an adequate description of what they see.

Eyes will see light of differing intensities, some described as shades or shadows, dark corners or hidden areas. They will also see multitudes of shapes and recognize which of them might be described as squares, rectangles, circles, etc. Even if their names are not known, shapes can be perceived through the impact of the whole or, because the eye can run along its periphery, as a unique impression of that continuous line however swiftly it be traversed.

Eyes will in every case recognize movement. Indeed to see is to perceive change. Change can be produced by the scanning of the eye (or the movement of the eye balls) on a static picture, or through the actual shifting against a stationary background of a moving part.

Because of experiences which we shall spell out more completely in Chapter 2, the combinations of light, colors, shapes, and movements will to varying extents provide impressions some of which men already have labeled (by such words as "design," "overlap- pings," "contrasts," "distortions," "perspectives") and others which we have not yet felt a need to label.

Because of other experiences, time sequences can be considered as alternations or alterations, these being in their turn abrupt or continuous, rapid or slow, rhythmic. Still other experiences enable one to decide whether visual impressions are exaggerations or under- statements, magnifications or reductions, as measured by man's scale of perception of nature or through some optical instrument.

This and much more is perceptible by ordinary eyes even if most viewers are not conscious of regis- tering such impressions. In a way, the ability to do this is the spontaneous contribution of the viewer to the image, offered without any prompting or demand. It is the gift of the viewer, taken for granted by every- one. (Seeing could itself be a worthwhile field of study, so as to know when features that we in igno- rance attribute to the image are in fact the "meeting place" of viewing and of the image and to know which of the two elements contributes what, and whether and to what extent, in regard to viewing, this contribution is made possible by the education of one's sight.)

3. These features of viewing go to form the image that appears on the screen and are each characterized by a continuous range of change, going from disap- pearance to total dominance; their multiple compati- bilities also permit the blending of a number of them in various amounts and ways. The attribute of infinity is thus one of the resources at our disposal in viewing —television no less than anything else—and this with respect to so many features of viewing that from the start we can suspect that the television medium is as flexible and as varied as nature, plus art.

4. Because what appears on the screen is chosen by

individual men, the element of art in any program will
depend on the techniques available and the consciousness of the contributing generation of artists. This
component is therefore historical and can change as
much as the imagination of the artists permits and
their daring and the social acceptance of the moment
allow.

Even when telecasting is live from nature, the way
the cameraman uses his tool brings back the artist and
his interference upon the subject being presented. In
the case of edited documentaries, it is clear that a
number of sensitivities, opinions, beliefs have acted
upon the content on cellulose to change mere "nature"
into "nature plus art."

The image part of the medium is as rich as man's
awareness of imagery and as varied as man's mind. This
is why we have maintained that the future of the use
of the medium is coincident with the education of telecasters in the use of themselves as people who can
reach the dynamics of seeing, imaging, and imagining,
and can find in the medium the infinities of uses,
known or still unknown, of man by himself.

5. So far we have concentrated only on visual images
that appear on the screen, in the minds of viewers and
of the producers. But sound is an inherent part of television. We shall consider it first by itself and then in
conjunction with images.

The sound from the set encompasses everything
that sound is: loud or soft, continuous or syncopated,
intense or dull, monotonous or varied, produced by
voices or instruments, guns, machines, engines, animals,
winds, sparks, and so on.

The sound part of the television set has a power
not possessed by the optical part, namely, it can reach
and affect an audience that is not facing the set.
Sound goes around obstacles that stop light rays.
Hence we can draw attention via the sounds emitted
by the set when we cannot via an image, however
beautiful and worthwhile. In sound we have a trigger

of a process that can later be taken over by visual images.

6. Because sound has as its support the surrounding air and because the air takes time to convey its messages, there are fundamental differences between the sound and the light components of the medium.

We have already noted that electrons have negligible inertia, while the inertia of the eardrums and the earbone chain is considerable. It takes much more intrinsic energy to convey a message to the ear than to the retina.

In addition, vision is in space and sound is in time. When we listen to speech, we need to wait until the end of each sentence to understand what is meant, while the act of looking at a landscape provides immediate and simultaneous information from an infinite number of sources. In other words, vision is essentially synthetic and hearing analytic, although through focusing we restore analysis to sight and through memory and conceptualization synthesis to hearing.

The difference between vision and hearing becomes critical when we try to relate vision to speech. In speech we use large muscles such as the tongue, and we are restricted to a certain degree by their inertia in our effort to increase as much as we would wish the speed of expression. Thus compared to the practically infinite speed of light, the speed of verbal expression and of hearing are so slow that sound can with difficulty become complementary to light—that is, vision. The slowest by necessity slows down the use of the faster, the case on television as everywhere else.

In the training leading to fast reading for example, the main obstacle to overcome is the use of the tongue to produce each word, though silently. Speed of reading is achieved when the eye rather than the tongue is functioning in the reader. Eyes normally take in chunks of reality. In fast reading, this property of sight is made to function again in place of the slower process of scanning word after word, line after line.

7.   In considering the use of sound on television, we must be prepared to distinguish very sharply between sound and speech. In so many of the current programs, speech is the deciding element. Hence most of the potential of the visual image is not made use of and is subordinated to "telling a story."

A sound system is a built-in element of the TV set. But it is not compulsory to think of it as being only a carrier of words or music. It may have much more to offer. These possibilities are likely to become clear once we stop thinking of sound as being mainly the medium of speech.

Sounds can be studied in themselves (and for certain purposes should be), as if we were blind people. Such a study would contribute an awareness of sound per se as well as an awareness of the various qualities of sound that our ear and our sensitivities can detect and register.

Sounds can also be studied as concomitants of some visual impressions and can be perceived as such when the sources of sounds are shown on the screen. This association will be important for lessons we will discuss in Chapter 3.

8.   The medium of television thus far has been looked at in terms of its fabric and found to offer a multiplicity of components that, as we shall see, can become the starting points of several new uses of the medium, some of which will be relevant to the tasks of education.

But the medium has already been explored by curious minds and led to uses that naturally have become part of the equipment of producers and directors. So many effects can be produced on the screen simply by making use of these facilities that even today, so early in the history of television, we can be confident that we can attempt miracles that can: fuse contradictions; bombard the mind with selected impressions; generate simultaneously or at chosen moments, impacts whose effects are calculated; force the mind to absorb what may never be met in one's life; enable one to discover the frontiers of one's senses and perhaps push beyond them so as to produce new dimensions for seeing, hearing, feeling, creating.

Since questions about the medium involve people acting on the components of the image, it is possible to look at television as evolving, like all other means of expression, by virtue of the fact that men continue to find more and different things in themselves, in their consciousness of themselves. For this very reason, one can see on television the use of the lecture, the drama, the concert, for which the set is a convenience only, and at the same time the use of all the innovations that belong to the new technology of producing effects on the screen and the space around it. What is television today may one day be seen to be as clumsy as the early Mack Sennett movie shorts. Yet the television of today will also be seen as something that is characteristic of man's knowledge of himself at present, for he does not show on the medium aspects that do not yet seem true to him and shows others that he finds acceptable. Television as means of expression is far more important than television as means of communication.

9. Because the medium of television is so interwoven with man's mind, one can be distinguished from the other only when the set is dead—that is, off—and has become an object that has assumed its static features. Indeed a television set alive is no longer a set: the image filling the sensory space of viewers forces them into dialogues that reduce perception of the set as such to a negligible minimum. To talk of the medium of television is in a way to talk of man the perceiver, the responder, the expander, and the processer of messages.

10. Producers and engineers as people belong to the category of viewers and as such filter the impacts of what is on and around the screen when it is alive. The medium never gains total independence, and viewers

never really experience electrons acting of their free
will on a luminescent screen. There are always minds
as part of the medium, and viewing is always to a
certain extent brainwashing.

11. In many instances, the showing of certain subjects on television may allow no time for editing and
no time for selecting viewpoints from which to shape
what is being imposed by circumstances. Instant trans-
mission of raw-life makes raw-life expression the object of one's experiencing, the experience of men experiencing whatever they are in. This experience by
proxy has shown its capacity to reproduce the components of direct experiencing. Man thus often becomes a witness, a close witness of raw-life for hours
every day. Consequently, he discovers his changed
place in the world. His need now is to process what
until recently he had to imagine—and only if he
wanted to and in the terms of his own choosing. Now,
it comes to him without much choice whatever his
disposition. He is "poisoned" by the insidious image
which he can no longer shake. He has to live the fate
of images. Their transmutation into trauma or delight,
into strong or weak emotions, into thoughts or opinions, may in a way no longer be his choice.

This is one way of understanding the current
popular phrase, the medium is the message.

The truth of this equivalence—between medium
and message—at the level of feelings has been known
to all of us. One knows at once that one is frightened.
Television, by reaching these levels as a matter of
course, can share the immediacy that is one of the
powers of feelings. But it is important to understand
that the equivalence occurs in a human being and
can so do only because the model for such equivalence
already exists in man's somatic system.

Speech, in all the situations where it can "poison"
the self, also shares the property of equivalence of
medium and message. Words in an unknown foreign
language obviously have no such power. But when

words are spoken in the mother tongue or in known foreign languages, in so far as they have access to the dynamics of the mind, they trigger as easily as visual images the feelings that give reality to the equivalence of medium and message.

12. The complexities of the self can be found in every one of its manifestations. Television is one of the ways of expression for man, and in it we can find as many of the components of the self that make this particular medium compatible with the source of expression behind it.

If man had no inner means that allow him to be in tune at once with what is susceptible of instantaneous change, there would have been no television. Television is the means man has developed so as to unfold the components of his self that are of this nature. The result is the new culture we are seeing blossom before our own eyes.

It is a new culture because man is cultivating what was in him but was not consciously required until the present. It is a new culture that will generate forms for each of the awarenesses he now will make explicit. Through these forms he will be better equipped, because more aware, to know what is compatible with the demands of the unfolding universe of experience and to reject what is incompatible.

Since the future is a process of unfolding, no one can tell what it is going to be. It will take all men and all their conscious moves to actualize the new culture. What this generation can do for the next is to open up opportunities. In no sense can this generation tell the next what to do with itself.

13. In the fabric of the medium of television there must be counted the existence of those people who explain what they believe it is. For their influence makes the users, in all senses, look at television as if it were what the explainers say.

As the writer of this book I know that what I am

doing with myself when I study the medium is becoming, in the final analysis, part of the medium. In a way, by injecting into the medium, through my readers, my vision of it, I am making the medium be different from what others have made it.

14. By including my eye in the medium, I have called in my sight and through it the culture that makes me aware of what to look at and what to turn my sight from. By including the culture in the medium, we open up two vistas: one of seeing the compatibilities between our cultivated sensitivities and what can be offered them by the medium; and one of casting away our preconceptions, our prejudices made explicit by the shock of the encounter of a true image and presumably true belief. Television, the outcome of one culture, becomes the beginning of another.

Man therefore finds himself face to face with his creations and has once more to make choices—passionately, because for some there is a blinding dazzle even if it looks dim to others, and inevitably, because the old culture has vested its interests in the new medium, not knowing it would be caught by these investments even when it hates the medium, while the new culture is suggesting new investments and paths to the visionaries and the believers (who, clinging to their investments, will become the conservatives of tomorrow).

15. The practical men now cling to illusions while the seers create the hardware and the objective forms that become the new culture, perhaps very different from ideals held for short times. This reversal of orders creates a sense of revolution, but in fact it is only life teaching men to live at peace with what is made explicit by the change of time into experience.

To close this section on the medium, we could not offer a better note than this equivalence of time with experience. Time is given man by life. But to live is to exchange this time for as much experience as it can buy. Television, using simultaneously *at least* two forms of time—the one that at the speed of light immediately changes reality into an image, and the one that unrolls a story at its own pace and the pace of speech—television is telling man that he may now, by his genius and knowhow, act upon the transformations and provide perhaps an economy for the exchange of time into experience that will move more and more experience from the present randomness to an understanding that is true to reality. This we are slowly learning via the complex medium of television.

Education today can be conceived as the study of this economy, of this exchange of time for experience where the tests, rather than being high fidelity reproduction of the status quo, of the static, are the number of transformations at one's disposal for generating a great deal of awareness out of the shortest impact.

Man does not need to prove to himself that his mind is dynamic—a cursory look at any of his functionings will convince him of that at once. What seems to be a new challenge to him is that, in becoming aware of his self, he is finding means of replacing the technique of looking behind his back at his past by looking at what he needs to do with himself to permit the future to act upon both the past and the present so that these gain significance and meaning for the process of living.

The theme of this book is that television has a role to play in making this awareness commonplace and according it its right place in the process of visualizing the future to help mold the present.

2.

Who Are the Viewers?

1. We all know that each of us has been a child and later an adolescent. We all know that during our adult life we are engaged most of the time in trying to make sense of events and the people around us, of our destiny, and so on. But because we are so absorbed in this task, we usually do not find time to ask the question: "What have we had to make sense of during the various periods of our pre-adult life?"

This is a key question, for it is valid over the span of one's life as well as over the span of cultures. We shall use it systematically, for it will help us reach an objective basis for offering a large number of television programs for various age groups.

2. Some of the facts of our lives are:

— most of us take from three to six weeks after birth to reduce our "need" for sleep from almost twenty-four hours a day to sixteen hours a day,

— most of us, when we are in our crib or even some time later, are not interested in becoming either President of the United States or married people or mathematicians,

— most of us spend around one year before walking and talking and take between one or two years to speak fluently,

— most of us first sit and stand before we walk,

— most of us walk before we run or jump,

— most of us learn to talk before we learn to read,

— most of us play some games during a particular time and stop playing them after that time,

— most of us, at certain stages, were unable to play with our brothers, sisters, neighbors or school mates, then found that we were, and fell out and fell in with them a number of times, but for different games,

— most of us acquire a doubt about our own ability to know by ourselves and also acquire a belief that to learn requires guides who are usually older persons or "qualified" ones,

— most of us became adolescent and stopped being adolescent but would not know why,

— most of us see in very different ways our past, our present and our future, sometimes even rejecting as invalid what we passionately have been,

— most of us are completely baffled by some occurrences in our respective societies while other people are not, and often what puzzles us at one stage seems to make sense at another,

— most of us are not aware of what we did with ourselves at different moments of our life,

— most of us guess most of the time what motivates other people to act even if we often find that we are wrong,

— most of us are unaware of what makes us feel objective or subjective about certain issues when they are examined,

— most of us tend to replace understanding by explaining (the former requiring an open mind, the latter a theory),

— most of us relinquish our critical powers under the pressure of "authorities" and use authority as an acceptable criterion of truth even against our own perception.

3. In front of every television set there are people viewing. From outside they all show two eyes focused on the screen. They are taking in something. Is it possible to find an approach that will tell us what?

Could we for instance ask viewers to communicate what is happening to them while viewing? Would a questionnaire which uses words and receives words, do? Would tests of basic metabolism be better, since they presumably indicate, according to a particular theory of man's behavior, whether some emotions are aroused and for how long? Would interviews—which would take ages and lead to answers difficult to compare and classify—be better?

Certainly, just looking at viewers from the outside would not provide us with any satisfactory answer to our question.

This is why we will try the approach that follows. It is based essentially on the inner workings of the self and can be translated into criteria that are measurable by the sort of objective components that are sought after by those who believe that physical behavior is the only real characteristic of the manifestations of the self.

4. If we watch ourselves talking, we can note that we have to move our lips, that our tongue is doing very many things so as to produce the very many sounds of our language. The question, "When have we learned to do all these things?" although it cannot be answered explicitly even in our own case, is certainly legitimate. When we note that like all children we were not born talking, we perhaps would be led to the approach of observing very young children and ask ourselves another question, "How do children make sense of what other people do with themselves when

they talk?" Or, put another way, "What are the means required to make sense of what is not observable in others, such as the movements of their tongue?" Here we are meeting two problems, one concerned with the perspectives of each of us as adults and one that is the actual challenge we are talking about, the problem of learning.

As to the first, since most of us do not ask of ourselves the question individually, we are satisfied if we are told that children learn by imitation and from there we go to some other questions, believing we already have been given a valid answer. A moment of reflection will bring forth the fallacy of this answer and force us into inquiring more deeply of the means available to children to learn how to talk, thus making us move to the second problem. The really serious one.

Since it is impossible to observe from the outside the movements of anyone's tongue and since we all learned to talk, the only conclusion is that we use means other than imitation to do what we see others do or use. At once this reflection brings to our mind the fact that children learn to crawl without seeing anyone around them do it. This kind of learning therefore must begin within ourselves for its own reason and go on until it has done its job. When it has done its job and this awareness is reached, we either stop certain behaviors like crawling, sucking our thumb, etc., or utilize their output or outcome for further explorations.

5. Growth can be seen in two ways: as a random sequence of accidental behaviors either picked up from the environment or forced upon us by the environment, or as a flexible variety of ways of integrating into one's system what is compatible with what is already there and can be articulated with it (*in toto* or selectively) so as to produce a new system which in turn integrates what is compatible with it and so on.

This second conception can itself be looked at in at least three ways:

— In the recapitulation theory, growth consists of the inevitable display by the individual of what the group, the culture, the civilization has gone through from time immemorial. In so far as the individual's system did this, it was guaranteed survival and progress.

— In the various conditioning theories, growth is the outcome of outside pressures, of pressures from the environment, which together mold one's behaviors so as to produce those that are acceptable to the group and enable one to perform the explicit and implicit ends of the group.

— But growth can be also seen for what it is, a succession of mysterious, complex, introvert and extrovert movements of one's self working sometime on oneself and sometime on the environment, making both changeable and capable of renewal. This is the view taken here.

The actual process of growth cannot be reduced to the biological model of assimilation and accommodation because man does prove every day that he transcends his environment and is substituting progressively a man-made universe for a "given" universe. The man-made one is in no way a necessary universe: it is actual, it is there, this is all. For instance, to think of Galileo in the seventeenth century extracting the concept of acceleration from reality (because the time had arrived when such knowledge was needed), even though men had always run down slopes in nature, is perhaps enough to suggest that today we may all be surrounded by phenomena that (for various reasons) we are not interested in perceiving.

To account for real growth we must have a model that continually corrects itself as man becomes aware of some dimension of his being until then neglected.

6. In this book on television and education, the most important of the neglected dimensions that we shall consider are:

— Each age has its meaning, its function in the process of making one's powers explicit and utilizable.

— Each person has potentially many lives to live but actually only lives one, his own, known if ever on his death bed.

— A period in which some power of the self is used extensively to the exclusion of others can generate a culture that is based on that power and is different from cultures that stress other powers. For example, television is stressing "knowing through the eyes," "a swift integration of impressions"; it is thus inevitably producing a man that functions in new ways—hence producing a new culture.

— Education relates the group explicitly to the individual and, by acknowledging the different significance of his successive ages, can provide the individual with means that accelerate some transformations while slowing or even stopping others. Education is helping to produce the change of cultures that men are witnessing and is not trying to stop it through opposition.

7. For each of us, from birth, growing up means the transformation of our system so as to perform what we could not perform previously and the integration into our system of what is new.

Thus immediately after birth we breathe, feed, assimilate, evacuate—things we did not do previously. We concentrate all our powers on them and close ourselves to all interferences. We do not see, nor hear, nor feel the outside world. All our time is devoted to learning—is, in essence, *changed into learning*—the vital functionings.

Only when to our satisfaction, we have mastered these functionings do we begin to shift our attention from our inner mechanisms to the problem of how to educate our sense organs. Hence the myelinization of our sensory nerves after a few weeks of intensive "catatonic" experiencing.

It will take years to educate our senses because

they are many and because no one chooses one's environment. Spontaneously everyone of us engages in the exercises that educate the senses.

From outside, these exercises look like games and usually are treated as games. (So, well-meaning but unfortunately ignorant members of the family will buy specific toys for special ages.) From inside, even the very numerous questions we have to ask ourselves as learners do not prepare us for all the occurrences we are likely to meet. We may for instance have spent time learning to use the same opening, our mouth, for breathing and for eating, and so we may know how to close our windpipe when opening our esophagus, but two years later we may have to relearn how not to talk while eating, lest we choke, since the use of one's mouth and one's muscles are different in each of these two activities. Or if one day we eat spinach that has not been sufficiently reduced in length, we may again struggle with a new use of the epiglottis.

Therefore, to have controlled our system for some activities is no guarantee that the learning is final and perfect. In some cultures adult re-education of breathing, learned in most cultures only for survival purposes at the beginning of life, is considered a useful way of awakening the self to many tasks left undone.

8. Our spontaneous learnings are models of what we can do with ourselves to meet some challenges. They are neither final nor the best. This is why educators of early childhood like Maria Montessori thought of taking every child far beyond what can be reached spontaneously in urban environments. Thinking of what a few people like acrobats, or members of particular tribes, can do with themselves should make it clear that even though our spontaneous growth far outstrips the gifts of our formal education, such learning is still but a very poor beginning on the road to total education. Even if we have learned from what we have done with ourselves, to face at the proper moment

the challenges of life, and to develop in all areas of experiencing functionings that are as smooth, as elaborate, and as swift as those of early childhood, we still have potential to unfold, as exemplified by those who specialize in some extra-ordinary use of themselves. If they can do those things, it just means the things are do-able. Today we may be prevented from generalizing such performances by our inability to reduce the cost in time and energy for obtaining them, but this may not be the case forever. The direction in which education is moving today may suggest that such reduction will be one of the tasks that can be taken up in the near future.

The course of our spontaneous learning tells us that as soon as we have achieved a mastery in some use of ourselves, we move at once to explore how to use this mastery. The masteries are achieved when necessary and this success takes us to the threshold of another world, a new world. Thus we master the dynamics of the muscle tone in each of the muscles we can reach, the voluntary muscles, at the time we find each necessary. We learn this, for instance, with our lips one, two, or three years before we decide to work on our evacuation sphincters because we need our lips to talk (we have already learned how to use them for feeding) but do not need our sphincters to express ourselves or be accepted by our environment.

(It is indeed a remarkable fact that almost every baby masters the enormous complexities of the mother tongue before he concentrates on the evacuation sphincters. Can social habits have something to do with this? Are children left unconcerned about their sphincters either because urination and defecation are counted as natural by all or because diapers are imposed on them?)

An interesting example of the superposition of functions upon one another when using the same anatomy can be found in the versatility of our hands.

As bones, tendons, muscles, nerves, and blood vessels, our hands are one and the same thing; but used for writing, playing a musical instrument, holding a weapon, dealing cards, caressing, etc., they are functioning so differently that life requires us to start each of these various apprenticeships from scratch.

9.   Obviously none of these apprenticeships is instinctual; they are all learned.

The essential consideration for us is this: we must consider television viewers as the complex human beings they are, capable of an indefinitely renewable education which leads them from one area of experience to another, in the course of which the individual first recognizes how to use what already is mastered of oneself to make sense of what is being met and then recasts it to allow for a new entry (thereby making his system a new field), and keeps on doing this until one finds oneself renewed because one has functioned and is functioning differently.

Viewers will meet the experiences offered by any new types of television programs in the way they generally meet life challenges and learn to adapt to the new learnings required so as to live with the challenges.

If their tools (mental, that is) are adequate for the meeting of the challenge, they will integrate it at once. If the tools are such that no way exists to bridge the gap between what one is and what is required of one, then either the event does not touch one at all or fantasy gets hold of it to produce myths. To illustrate the first we need only to think of the millions of people who as young children survive the horrors of wars and do not view their youth as having been impressed by the events of the wars. To illustrate the second let us think of the ideas men have had of thunder in all cultures before ours, which is the first to have had an insight into electricity.

10.   These examples provide us with the basis for developing a model of growth that can be very helpful if we want to relate realistically to people as a whole.

At each moment, life is structured for each of us as if it was made of three layers. One layer represents what we have integrated of life and includes events, experiences we have made sense of. The second layer represents the experiences and events we are working on, are so to say at our level though not yet part of our functioning. In this layer we place our passions, our investigations, our interests and involvements, consciously using the mental equipment included in the previous layer. Not all of this layer is clear and usable, but all is accessible. In the third layer we place that which does not yet move us, mobilize us; that which we do not feel we need to enter into so as to grow, do not need to become adept in so as to continue our living meaningfully. To use a metaphysical notion, it is the realm of that which is transcendental for us. We need to change ourselves before something in this layer becomes perceptible, and we do not feel any loss by not being in contact with it. Growth, in this model, can be looked upon as either the movement of the mind that makes us enter the transcendental and bring some of it into the second layer to be processed, or as the work on ourselves that permits the transcendental to affect our awareness of our own experience so as to help make it ready to meet the unknown.

11. In a cultural grouping, people are at different stages in the process of self-integration, and one and the same event will have a multiplicity of meanings according to how it is met and whether the tools for its assimilation are at work or not.

It is well known that members of a family looking at the same movie display a variety of reactions. Some can be frightened by an emotional scene which is neutral for others who can let the thought that it is a movie play its part, while some others will feel the struggle in themselves of the reaction to the scene and the rationalization (for this reaction) that is budding.

Some of us never succeed in holding at bay some emotions and are vulnerable to any reappearance of a trigger such as blood, or violence against animals or children, and so on. For these people there are areas of experiencing which seem inalterable however long they live.

We are thus brought face to face with the variables we need to understand more fully if we want to be true to viewers of certain ages, at certain stages of their experiencing. The correction of the insight will be demonstrated by the ability of programers to assist viewers to grow smoothly, i.e. to meet in the programs experiences that they can enter into, receive meaningful messages from, integrate in their mind, and because of all this make minds more capable of taking a further leap, of entering worlds that were not suspected, were somehow transcendental.

To see viewers as seekers, not as passive people to entertain, will help all those who are looking for how to use this gift of a medium that brings home life in the raw, not signs and symbols that one has to interpret.

12. To assist programers in their assessment of what particular audiences may be presented, with considerably high chances of being affected in a way that represents growth, we can go back to some observations hinted at in the discussion of what we make sense of at various stages of our growth.

Once a certain age group has been selected, the problem becomes precise.

Let us work on the class of viewers we may call preschoolers, the two to six year olds. This term of course is a misnomer since many children are at school at the age of four and more still at five.

More importantly, it is wrong to equate age and experience, for reasons we discussed earlier and can recast here in terms of awareness, as follows.

Never again do we become as involved in the challenge of speech as we are between the phase of nonverbalization and the time we master speech. It therefore is likely true that between the ages of one to three, say, we are best equipped to study the universe of speech sounds, and that later years would show us as having regressed in our capability of doing a really good job in that area. Though we are older, the mere passage of years is not equivalent to growth.

Awareness of oneself as being involved in certain experiencing serves us much better as a measure of growth than does age. To compare people only by age, size, weight, and other similar attributes, leads to trivialities precisely because the selected attributes are superficial.

The little ones are as legitimately living their age as older ones are, and the only question is to grasp what is meaningful to their level of awareness, since they do not care to verbalize it, at least not all of them.

Preschool children must be looked at as investigators. They do not explore at random, though they have to relate to their world according to their gifts, their tastes, their opportunities, and thus may differ considerably one from the other.

What they all have to do however, is use inner movements of their mind to make sense of the outer world, the world they suffer from, and are immersed in—the world that is not ruled by them as their inner one is.

Hence we have to look at children from within and from without. Behaviors will reveal the truth of their self *only* if the behaviors correspond to mastered stages, which cannot be determined from without alone.

While children move towards mastery, their behaviors need to be interpreted differently for different children and at different moments for the same child. Such interpretation needs on the part of the interpreter caution and imagination because what he sees being lived may be utterly rejected at a later point by the child who displays the behavior—at that point, to be precise, when the child has reached the proper criteria to guide his steps. To resemble children exploring their various universes, investigators of childhood need to cultivate among other things the suspension of judgment. Indeed, how can one meet the unknown with peace of mind if one invests in it? Children, at least young children, are at peace with their size, their lack of knowledge, the differences in performance displayed by themselves and older people in a variety of fields. This quality of mind tells us that they find enough to occupy themselves in what they are doing and have no need even to consider adding to themselves whatever might enable them to be equipped as their elders are or seem to be.

13. Between two and five most children must do the following: acquire speech; acquire the mastery of their body movements both for feeding themselves and walking among people and objects of various sizes and consistencies; learn to recognize the demands of knobs, doors, faucets, keys, etc., so they can use their hands for a variety of functions; learn to assess the variations of muscle tones which lead to different jumps, so they can lift themselves, swing, integrate various rhythms; learn to be sure of their judgment of sound, color, size, shape, distance, so they can shift judgment from one sense to another, so as to coordinate impressions and actions and recognize danger and how to face it with the adequate response; etc., etc.

If the list can be quickly made, the actual living of each learning experience consumes part of everyone's life.

The mastery of each of these things involves three steps: first, the recognition of what one is encountering; second, the acquaintance with it that leads to familiarity; and finally, the mastery over what has been met, which proves itself in the confident use of this mastery to enter into new areas and start again the cycle of recognition, acquaintance, and mastery.

Every learning in life requires this sequence if it is to become part of oneself and to function without a hitch. The analysis of children's games will confirm

the existence of this sequence at once to every atten-
tive observer.

Using our list of the activities with which children
two to five are involved, we can therefore look at
these children as viewers whose interest will easily be
captivated if we offer them:

— experiences that permit them to increase their
acquaintance with the world of sensations and mutual
play,

— experiences that extend their familiarity with
what they are engaged spontaneously in knowing and
mastering, such as the realms of sound, light, form,
etc.,

— experiences that use the mastered skills as spring-
boards towards the conquest of successive unknowns,

— unformulated experiences which spring in the
minds of creative people but can be entered into
directly without the preparation of scholastic study,
as may be the case in the arts,

— experiences by proxy contained in stories or
adventures that extend the realm of the actually feasible to the realm of the virtually feasible where make-
believe is the measure of the need to transcend the
limitations of the world in which one finds oneself,

— experiences which, starting with what everyone
has, take one to a metamorphosis of the world when
new powers are being endowed to one.

14. The presentation of these experiences in terms of
television programs will be done in the next chapter.

Here we can expand somewhat the points above
in so far as they enlighten us on who the viewers are.

For example, the activity of make-believe, which
is observable in children even before they are one, and
never leaves us, can be considered as one of the manifestations of the mind transcending the given world.

Still, in make-believe some components of reality are
scrupulously respected. Such respect requires that we
acknowledge that children are sensitive to the "logic
of things." This sensitivity describes their sense of
truth. To relate to them, we in turn must respect this
sense of truth, otherwise we shall lose the bridge of
understanding.

The best writers of children's books have such respect. Since we know how few stories over the centuries have remained in children's literature, we see
how difficult it is to be sensitive to what children need
to encounter in order to grow through make-believe.

Children view cartoons on television for hours.
Cartoons—though true to children because they are
wholly based on make-believe and action—display
stereotypes that are soon so predictable that viewing
becomes a game of beating the author of the cartoon
in the unfolding of the story, rather than an extension
of a power offered the author by his viewers.

Children's interest in commercials comes from another of the characteristics of growth. It is the only
type of material that gives the child an opportunity to
test whether his mind can exhaust the content of a
complex situation. No other program is shown as often
as are commercials, nor is any other so short and so
focused on one aspect of life. Children view commercials with eagerness not because of their content (bras,
cigars, trips, etc., which, for children, are transcendental) but because they are opportunities to learn
about one's self, one's memory, one's insights into the
form of a message, the way material is used to obtain
some ends, the order in which images follow each
other, the words that are used and uttered.

15. Viewing by viewers who have varying "logics,"
i.e. various ways of looking at reality, forms the real
raw material upon which we must concentrate if we
want to have a correct lead for our programs. The
meeting of the various logics with some appropriate
programs and techniques is already taking place—more

by chance than by science, because most of us have
acquired seeing very early in our life and have rarely
added much by growing old.

The opportunity exists for those who wish to take advantage of it, to study how we can use television to develop for all, as never before, the penetration of our insights. The key to doing this is to recognize that it is our minds that see through our eyes and that since our minds are indefinitely extendible, so will be our eyes, without any alteration of their anatomy or of the nervous system.

The proposals of the next chapters are a beginning of a contribution in this direction.

16. Though a few short paragraphs have been devoted to children of two to five, none has been devoted to the other ages. Some knowledge exists of what we make sense of during the successive periods of life called childhood, pre-adolescence and adolescence, pre-adulthood and adulthood, but to refer to it in any detail would have made this chapter far too unwieldy, particularly as we are mainly interested here in television and its place in education rather than in the meaning of life. The last chapter in the book may serve somewhat to fill the gap for those who wish to continue the study of men engaged in processing life for meaning, and how television might aid in the task.

3.

Television and Education

In this chapter it will be possible to test whether the previous studies are sufficiently advanced to permit us to make realistic proposals for programs that are both acceptable to television producers and directors and also effective with preschool audiences.

1. Obviously everyone who looks at television knows that no program can stay long on the air unless it is entertaining. From our point of view, this condition simply means that the members of an audience find that a program easily changes time into experience and that the experience resulting from this exchange is acceptable, is compatible with their individual levels of functioning in the area concerned.

Jokes may be told too fast or may refer to situations alien to an audience and thus lose their entertainment value.

A scientific enquiry may be entertaining if the presentation of it mobilizes the curiosity of viewers and keeps them in contact with the mystery of the studied area, thereby generating in them feelings which are genuine, even though they may be of awe or respect for what lies beyond their ordinary life.

It will be this definition of entertainment that we shall use in all that follows. Thus so long as we can induce someone to look and to keep him looking, we shall conclude that he is being entertained by what we are showing him.

As guides in our attempt to be entertaining, we shall:

— respect the means viewers use while viewing,

— respect the viewers' rules of participation, which we maintain are based on what they are making sense of at the stage they are in,

— leave a great deal of the expansion of the situations presented for the viewers to do on their own after viewing,

— involve each program, however short or long, in the realities of the various dialogues viewers have with the various universes of experience offered man.

That is: we shall keep each program linked with the senses, the emotions, the masteries achieved, and the functions the viewers are testing, all of which represents the past and present of the viewers. A hint of the future is provided insofar as more can be drawn out from every situation. To hint at the unformed, unlived, unlimited is to refer to the unknown, to the future, and thus is to be more realistic, truer to life, than is the illusory offering of complete coverage.

These characteristics we hope will be found in each of the programs we shall be sketching in this chapter.

2. Most television shows teach us something, are educational in some way. It is often said that children who watch television already know, when they enter school, much more than their schooling will teach them in twelve or thirteen years. One reason given for

this is that learning from books is so much more time-consuming than watching the unfolding of a process on the screen; another is that television is so much more vivid that it is more easily retained and recalled.

Rather than discuss this view, let us contrast knowledge and knowing, a point touched upon in the introduction.

The main difference between the traditional outlook on education and the one presented here is to be found in the vision of man as a learner. Tradition sees memory as the key faculty; our view maintains that for man to know he must become aware of some transformation in his self which he then relates to the rest of his self and to other realities in his universe of experiencing. We contend that he *cannot* know without such an awareness. Tradition believes that he knows if he merely remembers.

Whenever we accept the notion that one is educated if one shows great knowledge in one or more fields, we have to face the challenges of obsolescence in the sciences, and of having knowledge that serves no purpose. We need also to confront the fact that the organization of a high fidelity memory runs directly counter to our enormous capacity to forget.

The pressure created by an enormous output of ever-increasing numbers of scientists and scholars, by the daily discoveries that alter methods of work, beliefs, accepted conclusions, is forcing everyone into the only viable alternative to a dependence on memory—to learn to be self-sufficient, flexible, and capable of independently getting at the sources of information. In terms of individual functioning, this is translatable into: since knowledge is the outcome of knowing, we would do better to concentrate on the latter and produce the aspect of the latter that is relevant to the tasks we face at particular moments.

The act of teaching someone what we know, according to traditional terms, requires only that we tell it to him or tell him about it; in our new terms, the learner has to be sensitized to a reality in which he will perceive for himself what we found in it.

Vast amounts of time and energy are made available to learners when we replace knowledge by knowing because in knowing one does not aim at a retention that is the outcome of repetition. In knowing, retention is the proof of awareness. It is in this shift that we find the source of the increased efficiency of the learning that can accompany television viewing, and not in the change of medium as such from print to electrons. Looking is sharp in essence and since it is synthetic and expands simultaneously over a multitude of items, it never requires itemization, item-by-item retention, hence by-passes repetition and drills which are time-consumers par excellence.

This is the way of learning—that is, through knowing—that mankind has used everywhere and at all times before it has needed to structure and codify, to transmit by sign and symbol rather than by experiencing.

No one can deny that much of man's experience is his own and has never been formulated in any medium but consciousness. This experience is not taught but is acquired. Following the methods of such acquisitions, we are learning to offer a new education that is of consciousness, of awareness, and particularly of awareness of the self objectifying itself in worlds and ways of being.

Television can assist in restoring to everyone what everyone has used for learning those tasks that are essential in every life (but have not been considered as such in the perpetuation of cultures and social groups), tasks such as becoming the master of one's imagery, or of the inter-relation between the senses so that one sense can be used while another is not called for or is in some way hampered.

Because a new culture is emerging, one that is trying to reconcile what can be reconciled from among all the existing cultures, we are now looking at man as the maker of cultures rather than as their product, at knowing rather than knowledge.

3. The proposals that follow are only examples. It will be clear that constraints have been observed in developing them.

In order for the proposals to be acceptable, they must be easily executed with existing manpower and techniques. They must also be capable of a yield considered to be greater than their cost by all those involved so that the process can be continued and the television stations find it profitable to let such programs go on. They must have, built into them, the germs of extension and renewal so that they can feed the very voracious schedules of telecasting which, in the future, are likely only to grow, with increased individualized viewing and with more countries turning to television, and with so many more demands being placed upon education.

4. Indeed education is required nowadays: for executives of corporations (to master systems analysis); for foremen and repairmen (to shift from technology to technology); for the citizen (to understand the various calls on his earnings, his own impact on the environment as well as the reverse); for children (to prepare them for life); for senior citizens (to learn how to use their plentiful leisure time); for workers and employers (to understand their mutual interests and those of the community at large); for civil servants (to take a look at larger issues than the matters that come to their desks); for politicians (to acquire what is needed to serve best their constituents while serving the nation first); for religious people (to integrate their mission, which is to serve their church, into the fabric of modern man's quest for truth and for significance here and now); for housewives (to harmonize their womanhood and the demands of family life); for whole families (to curb selfishness and relate genuinely); for adolescents (to live intensely while

exploring the world of the self within and the offerings of the social world without); for fathers (to get their relaxation with their children by delighting in them and growing in awareness with them); for mothers (to see in the everyday of their children, the particular steps they are taking and why); for university people (to reconcile their own research and the needs of their students); for educators (to take more and more into account the actual gifts and powers of students in order to help them become autonomous investigators of some aspects of their world); for medical people (to recast their thinking so as to become able to look at patients as people, at pain as a useful symptom of a dysfunction, to follow-up rather than suppress and to reach the total reality of man rather than his body per se).

Naturally judges, engineers, and lawyers, among a host of others, also are in need of education to solve their problems.

Is this the all-encompassing viewpoint that readers, in thinking about education, have in mind, or are they thinking of the many narrower concepts which amount to discharging some traditional duty, such as making children know the alphabet?

5. In this book from the start, education has been understood as the cooperative effort of responsible people who took upon themselves the task of making more of their contemporaries conscious both of the immense potential in each of them and of the techniques that make us capable of changing time into valuable experiences—valuable to their owner, that is.

Readers must keep in mind that the complexities that we are considering here have always been with us, are with us now, and have to be tackled by the proper means, which, if need be, must be created. Our lives are complex, and the demands upon us complicated. If we learn to handle these demands properly, we may find ourselves enthusiastic in front of that with which the future will challenge us, carefree and well equipped for meeting the unknown—in contrast to the condition imposed by our present equipment of recipes born of the past, useful only for the reappearance of this past, exactly repeated.

Very many among us will then find life more abundant because we shall no longer fear change, the unknown, and will welcome the new that renews us.

6. Nowhere in this book have we considered the social stratification of societies. It is clear that in some educational quarters the main interest currently centers upon the "disadvantaged." In the perspective of the present work, "deprivation" is a social notion that does not necessarily translate itself into any handicap in the use of one's self for one's own ends. If the environment is considered to be everything, then no hope is possible; but if it is only one of the components in our lives and if the trauma it creates can be neutralized by the working of the will, we can keep our hopes up and work with all children as individuals and persons.

All of us have a relatively poor environment in comparison with the environments of the most privileged among us or with the one we can expect the future to offer ordinary people. Further, human beings have achieved what has been achieved in the history of mankind mostly in conditions far less favorable than those obtaining in U.S. slums. It is possible to exaggerate the consequences for education of handicaps and deprivation. It is also possible to see some wealthy Victorian homes as far poorer environments than the streets where so many of the sixty year olds of today have had their truer education.

Now, if we accept an educational ideal that attempts to give all children equal opportunities at the start, how can we guarantee that the opportunities would be taken up and that all children of five or six would start their school careers on the same white line?

All we can actually do, as adults responsible for education, is to think through both the opportunities we should offer and how to increase their chances of being taken up.

If, in developing television as an educational tool, we are true to the meaning of childhood, we will be meeting true needs and interests of the moments, and our correct insight will make viewers want to participate. But if instead we provide experiences that only may be needed one day in the future, we should not be surprised if viewers turn their backs to the screen and enjoy the games they create themselves.

7. The programs described from note 8 onwards have been put together in two types of series. First, we shall indicate how we could organize *horizontally* a continuing, daily sequence of one-hour shows for a few weeks of five or six days, so as to offer to viewers a number of differing exercises, all entertaining, all true to the medium and to children.

Then we take a number of fields of experience and treat each *vertically*, in depth, thus providing a pool of programs that can be cut and arranged to produce another set of weeks of programs like the first series, but this time leaving to producers and to students of the responses to these programs—the responses we call feedbacks—the subtle job of selecting the arrangement that best suits their own tastes and those of their audiences.

By presenting both series, we mean to indicate that there is no theoretical reason for choosing one or the other. For example, it may be a prejudice only, and not a truth, that viewers prefer short programs and many of them one after the other, as we have at present on Saturday mornings on most channels. It may be found, when analyzing actual feedbacks, that the intensity of experiencing some programs permits viewers to accept and want much longer programs—and that such a response constitutes one of children's realities, i.e. that however young, if they are interested, their span of attention is as long as needed to satisfy their interest.

For the purposes of the present discussion, we have developed the following programs only to the point of making our basic ideas and intentions clear. Much remains to be done in detailing the programs in full. But that such further development presents no special problems should be obvious from what follows.

Horizontal Programing
8. The conception of a horizontal program means that, using 5- or 10-minute segments every day, one can develop a study that may take years to complete and do this for a number of studies, and then put various segments side by side so as to fill one hour every day. For example, each daily hour of horizontal programing may include:

> 10 minutes of the study of some property
>   of light
> 10 minutes of the study of some property
>   of sound
> 5 minutes of the study of some property
>   of shapes
> 15 minutes of the study of some aspect of
>   the mother tongue
> 10 minutes of the study of some property
>   of number
> 10 minutes for a riddle, a puzzle, a story,
>   a game

If 12 minutes for commercials or announcements are needed, one can reduce each segment accordingly.

The specific horizontal programs given here are offered only as examples, as simple suggestions to show possibilities. In no way do they express a belief of the author that they should be structured exactly as he says. They are not the result of experimentation and an optimal formula. Rather, they are an exercise in presentation aimed at offering as much a priori assistance as possible to other people like himself who are engaged in discussing possibilities, alternatives, and content, for years of television programing.

These programs can be presented live or on film or video-tape.

9. *A Study of Some Property of Light.* For present purposes, we shall treat the study of light in the context of a short film so as to indicate:

— that the subject can be developed in 10-minute time segments,

— that the program is absorbing enough for at least the age group considered here to justify its use,

— that it is educational for at least this age group,

— that it can blend with the rest of the hour to make the whole an entertaining sequence.

An absolute object exists only as a thought; in physical reality, each object needs to be seen to be perceived, hence needs to be lit.

For this study, we use two approaches which can be followed on two successive programs or in one and the same according to the taste of producers. One approach is to film an object, say an egg, on which a white light becomes stronger at a rate that reveals the identity of the object only slowly because of the way the object blends with the background. (On color television, the same material can be shot using filters of various colors so that the egg appears and reappears in red, yellow, green, purple, or any other color.) The second approach consists of filming a familiar object from extraordinary angles that conceal altogether the usual views we have of this object.

What we want to convey implicitly in these films is:

— that to see is to look at the interplay of lights and the reflecting and absorbing surfaces,

— that the reality of any object is an infinite class of impressions upon an indefinite number of minds,

— that the uniqueness of objects is special constructs of minds, which need to abstract what can be conveniently labeled for the purpose of communication.

Although what we just said is a summary of what we all do all the time, it may appear as a shocking revelation. But if we ask ourselves why do all children feel the need to draw, and why painters spend their lives examining what it is to really see, we will recognize the lessons aimed at in such programs are meaningful for and entirely within the grasp of young children.

These films (each of which could be either a 10-minute segment or half of such a segment) *must* be speech-silent but not necessarily musically silent. While we can leave the decision about the latter to experimentation, we cannot agree even to *try* a concomitant verbal presentation, for we know that with a voice the distraction will be irresistible and the result will be the poverty of a remembered statement and not the wealth of the deep awareness that silence would bring about.

10. *A Study of Some Property of Sound.* A number of small objects, say, four of them, composed of different matter (metal, wood, rubber, glass) are shown so as to be recognizable by their texture even by three year olds. Then a number of surfaces—a plank, a sheet of metal, a pane of glass, a plastic tray—are shown first individually and then side by side horizontally on a metal frame.

A voice then tells the viewers to watch the sequence, to listen carefully, and to try to remember what they *hear*, since they will be asked to play a game soon after.

Then at intervals long enough to separate impressions, the four small objects are allowed to fall in turn on one surface, then in the same order on the next, and the next, and the next. Before starting each sequence, the objects are picked up by the hand that drops them. Only the objects, the trays, and the hands are shown on the screen.

This game is then to be played by viewers, alone or in pairs or larger groups. (If necessary, the program can provide illustrations of how this is done.) In pairs, while one viewer looks at the screen and sees the objects falling, the second turns his back to the screen and states which tray is being used and the order of the objects as they are dropped upon it. His partner tells him whether he is right or wrong, and takes his turn when the next tray is used. A lone viewer may close his eyes, tell himself which combination of object and tray he thinks it is, and quickly open his eyes to check his guess. The time taken between throws can make this possible. If there are more than two viewers, only one needs to be the watcher; all the others either close their eyes or turn their back to the screen. The guessing game can be played twice, the second time the order of dropping being different from the first.

The lessons implicit in this film and game are:

— that sound is produced when two objects collide,

— that the sound produced depends on the nature of the substance of the colliding objects,

— that the sounds are somehow characteristic of the substance, i.e. that wood on wood and metal on metal can always be distinguished.

More can be said, but we leave it for later.

11. *A Study of Some Shapes.* A transparent cylindrical glass contains a colored liquid up to one half of its

height. A device tilts the cylinder slowly in such a way that viewers know for certain that the tilting is not a trick of photography, e.g., a piece of scotch tape hangs straight down from an object above the glass and is attached to the outside rim of the glass. If the scotch tape remains straight, there will be no doubt that the cylinder and not the camera is tilting. As the glass begins to tilt, the horizontal surface of the liquid shows itself as ellipses more and more elongated, until the liquid reaches the rim of the glass. A reversed sequence brings the glass back to its vertical position. The sequence can be repeated with glasses of different diameters.

What is conveyed implicitly in these films is:

— that liquid surfaces are always horizontal,

— that cylinders have an infinite number of plane sections,

— that one of these sections is a circle (when the axis of the cylinder is vertical) and all the others are ellipses with two unequal axes,

— that by the tilting, one of the axes of the section diminishes while the other increases,

— that the largest of the ellipses is formed when the liquid is at the point of leaving the glass,

— that a similar story could be told had the tape been stuck somewhere else on the side of the glass, i.e. there are an infinite number of ways of producing an infinite family of shapes called ellipses.

12. *Some Aspects of the Mother Tongue.* On the screen there appears one at a time and placed anywhere, but written horizontally, first the word *is*, then the word *it*. After *is* appears, a voice says, "is," but only once, and after *it* appears, says, "it," only once.

Then a pointer touches *is* and then *it*, leaving time in between for viewers to have said *is* and *it*.

Then the rhythm of pointing increases until *it is*, as in spoken English, is the response. The pointer disappears and soon reappears to show rapidly *it is*.

(It is expected on the basis of past experience, that this scenario will be sufficient to obtain this response from most three year olds without additional voicing by the invisible teacher. If experiments prove us wrong, a small class of preschool children can be photographed at intervals to suggest to viewers what other children can do in similar circumstances.)

Then on the screen appears the word *at*, which again is voiced only once. Then a "double" *at* springs up from the first *at* and moves away from it and is joined by the sign *p* to form *pat*, and then the word *pat* is voiced once. *at* and *pat* are shown once again without voice, by means of the pointer, so that viewers can say them. After this, the pointer shows in order *is*, then *it*, then *pat*. Some viewers will produce by themselves *is it pat* but perhaps will not yet produce the form of the question as it is articulated in spoken English. A more rapid pointing would elicit this question: *is it pat?* A recorded voice of a young child can say this on the program to give viewers an opportunity to check their reading of the pointing.

Soon after the sequence, *it, is, pat* is each pointed to at a speed sufficient to elicit the affirmative statement, *it is pat*.

Going back to *is it pat?* the pointer follows with the answer *it is*. Here again a recorded voice can be used to confirm the correct reading.

The screen shows the four words—*is, it, at, pat*—in their arbitrary positions. A closeup then shows alternately *at* and *pat*, leaving time for utterance by viewers. Then the film shows *it*, and a second later a double of the *p* from *pat* leaves the word and runs to *it* to form *pit*. From *pit*, a double of *it* moves away. We now have on the screen *at, it, is, pat, pit*.

A moment later with *a* stationary, *t* and *p* simultaneously rotate around it, pausing for a short while to form *tap* and continuing to become *pat* and again

tap and again *pit*. This is repeated with *pit* producing
tip; alternately *pit* and *tip* are formed.

Then from *pat* a double of *a* drops far enough
below the word so as not to interfere with the movement of *t* and *p*. When *tap* is formed, a double is
detached to cover the *a* and produce *tap* over it. Simi-
larly with *pit* and *tip*.

Now we can use the rotations to transform the
two words *pat* and *tap* or/and the two words *pit* and
tip one into the other, always leaving a short interval
for the utterances.

The screen shows the words *at, it, is, pat, tap,
pit, tip*. The pointer appears to form in turn *it is, is it,
it is pat, is it pat, tap it, tip it*.

The screen is divided into two vertical strips; on
one side appears the previous screen with its seven
words; on the other the six statements above appear in
turn written with a light pen on six lines. The pointer
touches in a random order the six lines to elicit their
utterance from the viewers.

The lessons implicit in this film and its techniques
are:

— that conventional signs can be connected with
one's speech, i.e. a reading behavior,

— that intonation is a feedback mechanism indi-
cating comprehension,

— that by introducing pairs of reverse words, one
ensures from the start a condition for their distinction
and hence for their nonconfusion,

— that pointing at words displays a property of
speech, i.e. of being in time, which helps learners make
sense of the rules of speech and facilitates reading,

— that the animation used (which in fact exem-
plifies algebraic transformations already used by all
those who have learned to talk and therefore forms
part of their intellect) can only help viewers in the
larger task of mastering the written form of speech.

13. *A Study of Some Aspect of Number.* In this study, either two cartoon figures or two children can be used. (The first is more under the control of the producers.) One of the figures says rhythmically, "one, two, three, four, five," up to ten. The other responds by saying, "ten, nine, eight," down to one. While one figure talks, the other listens and looks on attentively. Then both say together "one, two . . . ten," and backwards. Then one makes a sign to the other to be silent and, with pauses between the words, recites the sequence:

one_____three_____five_____seven_____nine_____

The other makes the sign of silence to the first and says:

ten_____eight_____six_____four_____two_____

Then one signs to the other that together they should each say his own sequence:

one	three	five	seven	nine
two	four	six	eight	ten

Then they do this backwards.

The scene dissolves and is repeated with the sounds "one, two," up to twenty, and then backwards, "twenty, nineteen," down to one.

This oral game is then replayed by the two voices alone, while on the screen the figures corresponding to the numerals appear and place themselves—

1	3	5	7	9
2	4	6	8	10

so as to display the story of the game.

The lessons and values of this film are:

— that a set of noises that can easily be recognized, repeated, distinguished, form a well-ordered set,

— that the activity of sounding and of not sounding, which can be controlled by the will of learners, is sufficient to provide them with a deeper acquaintance with the set of numerals that one day can be called the separation of the integers into the odds and the evens,

— that because numerals are treated as noises to be uttered, the two opposite orders on the set can be entered into from the start and practiced without any difficulty from then on,

— that because the experiencing of a set is treated as an activity of the mind (which is what it is) the extension of the set provides no problem and so learners are given conditionings that enable them to make sense of the usual work with "numbers."

14. *A Story, Riddle, Game.* To complete the presentation of activities that are natural for children of preschool age, we can add a section to the program that can be an illustrated story or an active game or a puzzle. The variable is left to the programers who may be particularly fond of some kind of activity at which they or their friends excel. The choice of a story here is equally personal and incidental.

The silent story of the short watch repairman disturbed by a burly unwanted customer, can illustrate how it is possible to put on the screen a story that displays a number of expressions of feeling immediately recognizable to young people, and to present them with an acute conflict of interests generated by chance and mounting into two crises. The story shows two worlds incidentally affecting each other and the aftermath of the battle of the minds involved, when one individual leaves the field in despair.

The little watchmaker, his magnifying glass on his left eye, was busy repairing a small watch. He did not hear

the doorbell ring when the door opened and closed.
He was trying very hard to finish a job in an hour for
a customer who was leaving town shortly. Now in the
shop waited a big, burly man who wanted to be attended to, but nobody came to serve him. He waited
a few minutes and got impatient. He called loudly:
"Is anybody there?" The watchmaker jumped in his
seat, and his tool, with a tiny screw clamped in it, fell
on the floor underneath a heavy cupboard. He looked
up and saw that the man was getting angry; he looked
down to see if he could spot his tool, still keeping his
magnifying glass on his eye. When he looked down,
he felt very unhappy since he needed the tool to finish
the job, and had no other. When he looked up, he felt
still more unhappy since he saw that he had to give up
his task and try to serve the big angry man.

It was not his job to attend to customers, his job was
to repair watches. But his uncle, who ran the shop, had
been called out and had not said when he would be
back.

The watchmaker slowly got up from his seat to go to
the counter. The big man stood there looking fiercely
at the little, slow watchmaker, who was as white as a
wall and, with his magnifying glass, looked like a one-
eyed snail. The two men said nothing, but thought
much. The little man wished the big man had not
come to trouble him in his work. The big man wished
he did not have the snail-man to serve him. He leaned
forward over the counter as if to grab the little man,
who took two steps backward to escape his grasp.

All this took a few seconds and then the big man
changed his mind, turned round towards the door and
went out, leaving the door open, the bell ringing, and
the little watchmaker baffled, standing motionless and
unable to figure what to do next.

This story was selected because it is so visual and
expresses a clear-cut interference of two time sequences represented by the separate involvements of
two people, one in what he is doing and the other in

the expectations he has when entering a shop to buy. It is also comic and distressing, baffling in its simplicity and full of insights into people and human relationships. Producers can make it teach a great deal by a perceptive use of the camera to show expressions of emotions that are much more suitably presented by the camera than the pen.

15. *Summary and Comments on the One-Hour Program.* One challenge in developing these segments was: Can we easily find material to put in one-hour programs that first are true to children of two to five in that they meet their spontaneous interests, can be made sense of by them, and have the capacity to captivate them, and second can be made so as to be shown on television? This has been answered, at least on paper.

Another challenge was: Will such material form an educational program that can be shown in all homes and serve growth?

The particular lessons emphasized and learned in each segment of the hour program tell only part of what can be made explicit by a succession of such programs. There is no doubt that experiential and intellectual growth can follow, and not only for the preschool viewer.

It is easily calculated that there are 120 permutations of the six segments described, hence 120 different presentations of the material. This in itself represents a dimension of flexibility that is important to producers. Further, even if one did stop at what has been written above, we already have more than one program by using variations on the themes. For example, the egg can be replaced by any number of other familiar objects (a spoon, an ashtray, a can . . .), the cylindrical glass by boxes of various shapes, the sound of falling objects by that of extended strings struck by a bow (or by that of a thumb on stretched fabrics), the given words by another set, and the transformations shown replaced by others. The number properties exemplified could be developed to give rise to others. The story is obviously one out of many.

In the next programs, each study will be taken further.

It is therefore clear that we could get scores of one-hour programs and that they could be written up in as much detail as was the one developed here. But in the following pages, another line will be followed. The next group of notes is concerned with what we shall call vertical programing and seeks to give hours of filming in some of the experiential fields we want to offer to viewers. Because of the bias that is ours, the presentation will include not only the material to be covered by the programs but also the techniques that can generate additional materials for many more hours of significant educational experiences.

Vertical Programing

16. In this section we shall allow ourselves to examine at greater length some subject matter selected for the horizontal programing above. A mixture of the activities in nursery schools and kindergartens (where the interests of students decide the individual schedule) and the concerns of scientific writings (which respect traditional presentation) has been selected here as the basis for the general content of the programs.

It is clear that vast amounts of knowledge available will not be used and therefore that very many alternatives exist from which to select any number of programs.

Readers should not judge what follows from their own particular vantage point of interest, for had this been known it is most likely that some sequence could have been found to satisfy it. Are we not looking at the whole of the universe and its forms and mysteries? In concentrating upon the forms that have a direct impact on our open senses and in organizing those forms so that

— the impact is maximized,

— the likely experience of the viewers is taken into account,

— the content is significant,

— the recall easy,

— the learning immediate as well as capable of being enhanced by the other involvements of viewers (during both waking and sleeping hours),

we are making a proposal that should be examined and criticized on these many grounds rather than on the readers' existing tastes and beliefs.

Vertical programing is another name for an unrestricted development of an idea or a vision. As before, so that the text remains manageable, we shall focus on general outlines rather than thorough descriptions.

Though the order of the notes that follow could correspond to the order of the appearance of their material in the horizontal programing, we shall not let this artificial consideration of separate segments control our discussion. Television programers would in any case use such material with different criteria in mind.

The detailing of these programs will amount also to a draft project of how to use television to solve a few educational problems.

17. *A Study of Sound.* This can be subdivided into:

— a study of noises

— a study of the attributes of voices and speech

— a study of music

— a study of notation

— a study of musical instruments

— a study of rhythms and movements.

We will examine most of these in turn.

NOISES. In the study of noises, the sound side of the television set provides the actual material that the viewer is to know and to recognize, while the screen provides clues that are concomitant to the sound and can by themselves establish the criteria for recognition.

Attributes of noises are classifiable in categories ranging from just perceptible to very loud, from continuous to unpredictable, from attributable to mysterious, from complex to singled out, from distant to on top of one, from threatening to soothing, and so on.

Noises become sounds when they are either perceived as attributable to some definite source or as having properties perceivable per se. This transition from noises to sounds permits the analysis by the mind of new dimensions that can in turn be studied before further properties are either deliberately introduced in the sounds or perceived to belong to them. Sounds are subsequently organized, contrasted, blended, produced at will by different means for special purposes.

The study of noises can be produced in a number of different programs of varying length.

i. A crack of close thunder followed by the noise of moving trees in a storm, the siren of a fire engine rushing to a fire, a jet plane taking off, a building collapsing, an avalanche, a blast-off from a rocket site, and many other loud noises can be heard with the concomitant spectacles on the screen.

One noise heard by itself and followed by a flash of some scenes shown before could then serve as an introduction to a matching game. Various modalities are available. Each of the noises heard in a sequence of noises (at first two or three, later five or six) can be repeated by itself out of order from the sequence while the screen is a blank, a second of time or so is left for recall, and a picture is flashed either of the source of the noise as seen previously or of some other source incapable of producing that noise.

Obviously we can remember noises and relate them to causes, though we are unable to communicate precisely what the noises are to anyone who has not lived through the experience that provided this particular substance and meaning. We retain a token of the noise, not the noise, and we are able to match this token with the noise when experienced; this is what we call recognition. Here of course the knowledge acquired by viewers is experience, but one which is not equivalent to the reality that affected us; their experience is of a symbol of the reality. We all know the thunder but cannot produce its noise.

If a noise is recognized as that of a sanitation truck processing the garbage emptied in it from some large can, the noise triggers the imagery and the understanding of what went on, never the ability to make the same noise. Thus, in stimulating such associations, we provide situations that enable viewers to distinguish between experiences and accept as valid both those that can be expressed and those that are inexpressible. The games proposed here will be providing the kind of checking experiences that may be needed as reinforcements for such perceptions.*

ii. Noises made by all sorts of household items can be used instead of the noises in *i*.

iii. Engines of different makes, parts of a car (doors, windshield wipers, air conditioners, fans, etc.) can form another set, for the study of specificity, loudness, etc.

iv. For the preschool age, pans and lids may be used to relate noise and size, noise and action, noise and kind of metal.

v. Thunder can be recorded to link noise and dis-

---

* *The programs could also be used to measure learning by a variety of formal tests. To make sure that images are correctly associated with their concomitant noise, the viewer could say a word that was sufficient to define the image; the retention then could be considered as having taken place. Likewise, if there were buttons associated with stills showing the corresponding scenes, depressing the right one would be equivalent to saying words. But this kind of control of learning does not seem needed by most living people, hence educators should give it up.*

tance, level of noise and darkness of skies and kind of storm, and perhaps even the approaching or receding of storms.

vi. A recording of a variety of moving objects that make specific noises, such as trains, ambulances, planes, could serve in an incidental manner to bring to the viewer's notice how pitch differs when moving objects come closer or go away from an observer. Such lessons could provide very casual introduction to the Doppler effect.

vii. Obviously all these recordings can be coupled with a number of games. There is neither need for specific instruction in such programs nor reason to feel that the lessons to be learned from exposure to them will fail to be realized—for they duplicate the spontaneous way used by all of us in acquiring experience. A cursory look at people in the streets will show that, like any reader, they have made good use of these lessons.

VOICES AND SPEECH. These can form a most interesting series of exercises on television for everyone, including preschool viewers.

Because we work for so long on our voice and that of other voices during our apprenticeship in learning the spoken mother tongue, we are already experts in our first three years of life on what voices are and can do. The awareness accumulated during this period constitutes therefore both the rock on which to build new awarenesses and the set of criteria we use for their study and classification.

Every voice is almost unique, but most voices betray:

— whether they belong to children (girls or boys) or to older people,

— whether they are speaking as natives or as foreigners either the tongue of the viewers or another,

— whether they are being used to express a casual thing or anger or supplication, a polite sentence, an order, a challenge, a threat, a sarcastic remark, an apology, etc.,

— whether they are used for talking, humming, singing, or for coughing, whistling, etc.,

— whether they whisper or shout, and while still conveying meaning, are speaking at speeds different from the slowest possible.*

A recording of forty or so languages can be used to convey the notion of: extremely different types of languages (in tone, syncopation, flow, and length of words); the families of languages (Romance, Semitic, African, Indo-European, etc.); and the various melodies of some phonetic characteristics.

Using such material, vast numbers of programs can be generated around recognition games. If voices alone are heard, it may be more difficult to place a particular speech than if at the same time people in national dress are shown on the screen. At some stage, if maps are utilized, the location of the people speaking the various languages could be used for games of association that connect voices, the speech used, the appearance of the speakers, the place on the map where they live.

One game may be the naming of the country or the speech of a series of individuals using the same language (here English) as foreigners. Identifying characteristics include not only the alterations resulting from giving different values to the sounds but also those resulting from melody, from stress and intonation.

This game plays with such questions as: Would it be possible while listening to a short conversation in English, to tell whether the speakers are Arab or Greek or French, etc.?

Another series of studies could be built around requesting each of, say, ten people from ten areas of

---

* *Speech on tape can be affected by a continuous alteration of the unwinding speed. This will show the various losses of attributes of the voices recorded.*

the world—who have been shown learning from a native a short song in a language foreign to them—to sing individually and without the native what all were heard singing (quite well) with him.

MUSIC AND SPEECH.　What viewers of two to five years of age will bring to this study is their readiness to experience the various components of music. They can listen and hear. They can be physically moved by the impact of beats and rhythms. They can easily retain melodies and even words, though not necessarily put the meanings to the words that coincide with those assigned by adults.

Hence in the study of music, the work can still be one of acquaintance and association, of distinction and assimilation, extending over a very wide range of manifestations of what mankind calls music.

For instance, as with voices, it is possible to classify instruments with respect to the range of the sounds they produce. Criteria here are easily produced by the qualities of impacts for which our ear seems to be structured, retaining at the same time the experience and the awareness that accompanies it. Voices can be re-classified as low and high (not necessarily being labeled as such by a voice on the sound track) by simply becoming aware of the component that (when notation is introduced) can be called "height." Mother's voice is generally higher than that of men, while brother's voice may be as high as that of sister.

When the ear is struck by sounds produced by various instruments, there is already in it a frame of reference with respect to "heights," even if all other properties of the sounds produced have not yet been isolated.

As usual, when proposing music programs for young people of these ages, we should constantly have in mind what they have achieved in the analysis of sounds and should refer as often as possible to what they have learned about synthesizing breathing, articulation, utterance, listening, hearing, the control of utterance of sounds through the ear, the judgment of emotional content of voices by the presence or absence of certain stresses, certain alterations of voices in terms of speed of utterance, and the production of sounds usually left out (such as shrieks) when communicating normally.

Keeping this in mind, we can propose programs that will lead to deeper awarenesses of both music and speech. Our method will be to explore the components of speech that are normally used in music.

i. For instance, most of us are not aware of the duration of words we use, even though speech is in time. Duration is cardinal in music, and the time structure of a melody characterizes the melody very clearly even when all other components are left out. Thus the tapping of a *sequence of noises* made with a pencil on a table tells at once which tune is on the mind of the tapper, if we know the tune.

ii. Besides the durations in a tune, there are notes. These are different because the number of their vibrations vary between 16 and 40,000 per second. The height of a note is the quality that tells how high the number of its vibrations per second is and conversely. Further, when two notes are compared, the ratio of the number of their vibrations is called the "interval" between them. One note is the "octave" of another if the interval is two. The word octave also covers all the notes between two notes whose interval is two. Our ear can perceive less than twelve octaves.

Voices may fall between any two notes of this "spectrum." The word "register" is used to describe the part of the spectrum that each voice can cover. Most voices start and end at different notes, but registers overlap and it is possible to classify voices roughly in seven groups. For men, the lower voices are called "base," the middle "baritone," and the higher ones "tenor." For women, the lower voices are called "alto," the middle ones "mezzo" (or "mezzo-soprano"), and the highest "soprano." Some men's voices overlap with those of women to form a category between tenors and altos called "countertenor."

Programs (easily designed) can be produced to convey this classification and can use games to make sure that the viewers correctly classify each voice they hear.

iii. Reference to the voice will convey that the energy content of each sound is also a variable, that we must use more of ourselves to produce a loud sound than a whisper. This attribute of sound, involving awareness of energy, leads to the idea of the "intensity" of a musical sound. Having people attempt to say every word of a sentence at the top of their register, rather than at the level of their normal speaking voice, will easily convey to them the experience that a greater expenditure of energy is needed to do this.

From this exercise, we can also grasp what happens when we listen to sound. When we hear a tune, we are bombarded with pellets of energy, and we respond to them by adjusting much or little, according to how little or how much the previous preparation of ours corresponds to the demands of the bombardment. We are all used to a certain level of noise or of sound. Any variation either way requires adjustment. Of the two sorts of adjustments, up or down, those towards the higher levels cost more because the energy required for it or received from it is greater than for adjustments towards the lower levels.

This explains why shrieks mobilize us at once and why we must concentrate in order to hear whispers.

It is easily possible to produce programs to study our responses to the variations of intensity. These programs will also serve to acquaint us with the way emotions—which are energy within the soma—are worked on from the outside, through variations in the intensities of sounds, and how from within they express themselves through the level of the sounds used to warn others of their existence.

iv. Finally our voices produce a luxury of additional sounds and become unique precisely because of the composition of the sounds uttered. In so far as the additional sounds do not obscure the intonation, do not interfere with the message the voice wants to convey, they are tolerated. Their presence is acceptable by the utterer so long as they do not distract. That they do not means that the energy content of these tolerated sounds is under control.

The general impact of these additional sounds is formed by certain "fundamental" notes and all those notes that agree with them, called "harmonics" because of this. The whole is called the "timbre" of the voice. We are all at peace with this state of affairs and accept the presence of all the harmonics in a voice as an additional guide in our dealings with others. Uniqueness of voices is indeed a very convenient attribute to distinguish among the many people surrounding us. Programs should also deal with these matters.

Thus far we have found that sounds have four attributes which are variable: duration, height, intensity, and timbre. It is possible to play variations on each of them and on any combination of them. This will transform the already numerous possibilities of combinations for one voice into an infinite number of possibilities of the use of sound generally.

From this analysis, it seems possible to offer television viewers experiences that will make clear that there are four components of sound on which mankind has worked and from which music in various cultures has selected special forms.*

Sound so far has been studied from voices because almost every viewer has one. We now move on to invented instruments.

---

* *The author has devised a new notation for musical sounds which not only is much simpler than the traditional one, and therefore preferable for beginning students, but also is more telling and more accurate. This system of notation is discussed in Appendix A. Here it is enough to say that, in contrast to the standard form of notation, the new form uses symbols that at once communicate their meaning to viewers.*

MUSICAL INSTRUMENTS. There are wind, string, and percussion instruments, and all of them are variations on the same principle. Programs can begin by presenting such insights as:

— taut strings when displaced from a stable position produce movements that even if they cannot be seen with the naked eye, can be heard,

— to blow in a cavity may produce a sound,

— to bang with a stick on a distended hide may produce a sound.

Then, fanlike, the programs can follow this up with a series of investigations: How does the nature of the material affect the sound? What do the dimensions of the instrument contribute? What is the role of the instrumentalist?

From the results of these investigations we can survey the hundreds of musical instruments and, first, grossly distinguish string, wind, and percussion instruments from each other. Then we can examine what makes the various instruments in each category different and develop guessing games—these are in fact games of recognition—that will enable every viewer to develop criteria within his hearing apparatus that will permit him to name which of the (unseen) instruments is being heard at that moment. It is obviously very easy to produce scenarios for legions of games that can lead young viewers to own the spectrum of experiences that will make them certain of knowing which instrument is being played.

From the distinction of instruments one from the other we can pass onto the study of how the register is produced on each and so set the foundations for classifying notes on one instrument and also between instruments.

It is easy to conceive of programs devoted to the production of sounds on instruments so that viewers acquire the certainty that they hear the same notes regardless of the timbre, or that they are hearing two or three or more notes and that one is the octave of the other on the same instrument, or the "octave" of octaves. Such programs will provide experience in depth and finesse in areas that correspond to what the very young viewers are doing with themselves at that age. Watching them tap and bang will soon convince everyone of their serious interest in such matters.

Octaves can be replaced by other intervals and various instruments can be used. At first, the use of one or two may be sufficient to establish the significance of the game. Finally, when enough variations have been experienced to guarantee recognition, the simultaneous use of musical notations on the screen (the form of these notations is discussed in Appendix A) and the sounding of all sorts of combinations of notes, can serve as a test of mastery. Such a game can show that viewers can be educated via television to absorb experience of sound on a spectrum much larger than is ever attempted without the means of television, and can be educated to make sensory judgments via the matching of symbols visible on the screen and sets of sounds heard.*

It is not at all optimistic to assume that most children presented with such a wealth of analytic and synthetic experience will as a result have found:

— things to listen to that correspond to their needs and are akin to what they spontaneously attempt in whatever environment they find themselves,

— that just by the activity of listening, they have formed criteria that are innerly tested and classified and can be used to recognize immediately a whole arsenal of man-made instruments,

---

* *It is conceivable that viewers registered with a program could be given workbooks with numbered items, so that evidence could be gathered by researchers wishing to evaluate this type of education.*

— that by examining the field of musical sounds charted and organized at first with full responsiveness to its nature and attributes and then, via notations, through visual means, they can substitute for some temporal data a spatial organization susceptible of increased effectiveness. (Because a notation system is permanent, it can serve again, while sounds unrecorded are lost.)

RHYTHMS AND MOVEMENTS. Here we shall use a mixed way of presenting the material. We shall have on the screen audiences of children filmed while they practice the exercises that the programs offer, our expectation being that the children at home will be inspired to go through similar movements.

In thinking about the substance of these programs, we must distinguish rhythm from meter and beat. The first is the response of the totality of the fluid content of our soma to the totality of the *continuous change* of the energy that stretches over the whole duration of any melody. Rhythm is a temporal attribute of music. Meter and beat, on the other hand, is a regular pulsation imposed on time. Beat is the superimposed *energy variation* that modulates rhythms by creating nodes upon the continuum of time, showing that it can be structured in many different ways. We notice beats first in a melody because they represent considerable variations in the energy content of our whole soma. But since time is the substance of music, and life is another temporal phenomenon, the incorporation of a melody (when we listen properly to music) *is a change of life-time into music-time*. The music-time remains available in the soma as a reproducible musical experience that requires as much life-time as before to be objectified but which nonetheless is recognized as different from life-time precisely because of the attribute of rhythm. Beats by themselves require the life-time of a rhythm to become a melody. When we hear beats, *we* fill in the gaps and so also have the rhythm, which we can supply only because we al-

ready have it. Otherwise tapped beats remain noises,
and whoever does not know the melody that is
thought of by the beater cannot produce it within
himself.

A melody has rhythm, meter and beat, notes and
some other musical components, but only rhythm and
meter act upon time (as if time were a substance), the
substance of life. Time of life can be structured simultaneously by superpositions of rhythms or/and beats;
cacophony results when some of these contradict
others and unison when some agree with others and
go to form a new rhythm.

The numerous possibilities of rhythms and of
beats can always be increased because of the capacity
to combine compatible uses of the soma. This permits
an indefinite renewal of music and dance.

Our soma responds to rhythms by externalizing in
forms and movements that reflect rhythms which are
within.

A conductor though only moving his hand or a
baton does this in time to convey to trained people
one of the forms in which one soma, his, is affected
by one rhythm so that these people can find how to
affect their individual somas in order to affect its functioning, this time for the purpose of playing an instrument.

Likewise a group of children listening to music
will have their soma affected by the rhythm and the
children can exteriorize this by moving their heads,
or their necks, or their feet, or their legs, etc., according to the rhythm or the beat. This is because of the
economics of energy: energy from the instrument
affects energy in the soma.

A class of children shown on the screen listening
to music need not be taught to respond to the music.
The children will respond naturally because they have
a soma that "creates" music through the awareness that
they have the capacity to structure time. Children if
asked to let rhythms move them, at once find expression for them in what their soma does: move, dance,

clap, tap, etc. Therefore, no matter what rhythms or beats we imagine being offered on the television programs, we can expect that viewers listening will show they are affected in the same way as the class of children being shown on the screen.

What the programs will do is give children the opportunity to structure time, to become aware of how many different ways exist for the soma to respond to rhythms, and to recognize different types of rhythm and their corresponding organizations of the self. These things children will learn, not because they are told that it is necessary for them to do so, but because the opportunity has made it available.

Children will even be able to retain words associated with their new awarenesses and will end up having analytic verbal knowledge where they before had only somatic knowledge and inarticulate awareness.

A typical program could start with a melody that is selected because its beat is distinctive and forceful.

Children would be asked to listen to it quietly and in a relaxed mood. The melody is played again; this time they are asked to hum it as they listen to it. A third time, they are asked to let their hands or their feet "follow" it. When this happens, obviously a transformation has taken place, and we must grant the children that they have transmuted something heard into a somatic expression. And once we grant this, we can ask for all sorts of single and combined somatic expressions—their heads, their right-hand index fingers, their left big toes, their whole legs at the hip, their hands and their feet (four combinations), these combinations and their heads, their torsos or a hand and the vocal system, and so on.

Clapping is another of these expressions. Marching and contorting one's body others. The movements of one's eyeballs and one's neck two more.

It will be left to the actual designers of the programs to select the rhythms and beats from the folk music of the world and to select also the particular associations between each of these and the various somatic responses, all to reach as rich an arsenal as possible of expressions of music.

Singing is obviously one form of somatic expression. It too could be added to the list of ways of showing somatic responses to what musicians put in their published melodies after their own whole soma tells them that the melodies agree with their way of perceiving their world.

The basic method of the programs has the object (and the virtue) of making every viewer into a person who not only will have listened to music selectively and extensively but will have investigated rhythms of the world with his whole being and achieved total immersion.

18. *Teaching Reading by Television.* Since the image on the screen can be acted upon by will and made to follow the instructions of a programer and since the sound part of the set can also be used at will, we may find that teaching reading is more effectively done on television than anywhere else for all but a very small minority of children. In this section we shall outline programs that could be tested at once and independently of all the other considerations that fill the pages of this book.*

All we shall require from our viewers in our effort to teach them reading is:

— that they view as usual,

— that they can talk at a level which permits communication with other members of the family,

---

* *Those readers who already know this writer's studies of reading in a number of languages may find it interesting to compare how this approach differs from the published one in that many of the tasks previously left to the decision of teachers are now delegated to television and its tremendous powers. In the United States, the trademark of the materials and techniques for teaching the reading of English is* Words in Color.

— that they can make sense of the voice or voices in the program.*

We shall not consider as a necessity that each viewer obtain books and materials to complement the television program. The exercise we are posing here is: can we thoroughly teach reading to viewers via the medium of television alone? Readers are invited to take in the full proposal as described below before they let their own experience of learning how to read —experience associated with other media—propose objections. As an author of a reading method for the classroom, the writer could easily have let the opportunity of meeting the challenge of teaching reading through television pass him by. But since he believed there might be something very important to learn here, the writer has sought to surrender to the medium all the medium can do to viewers, to discover whether viewers can end up by being readers no different from those who mastered the skill via other means.

Readers of this book can examine for themselves:

— whether the treatment that follows restricts itself solely to using television,

— whether reading for all results from this treatment.

Affirmative answers, we can surmise, will be of tremendous consequences in the worldwide struggle against illiteracy.

All we have at our disposal is: a screen on which electrons can be commanded to organize themselves

---

* *One part of assuring this is for the station to provide voices of people who use the mother tongue in the way the prospective viewers do, instead of in the manner of so-called "standard speech." The existence of the latter variations could be considered a refinement to be brought to the readers' notice after they have learned to read, so to speak, their mother's (not mother) tongue.*

according to our wishes for as long as we wish; color on color tubes; various hues of grey on the older black and white tubes; a sound system that can be used to convey the sounds we select for as long as we wish.

Almost all viewers who have acquired their mother's speech have alertness and mental plasticity. They have experienced make-believe from their first year and hence have a highly developed capacity to produce symbols and a sense of convention, of which the labeling of categories is one. Anyone who has learned to talk knows:

— that nouns cover classes of beings, verbs classes of actions,

— that the same words used by different speakers refer to different notions (pronouns, adjectives, adverbs),

— that the order of words is meaningful and is to be attended to,

— that this is likewise true with the order of sounds in words (*cats* and *stack*, or *cats* and *cast*).

Hence every viewer is far better equipped intellectually speaking than he would be if he were endowed only with a memory. Indeed, using memory alone for learning could make mental activity impossible, as we can see at once when we try to remember words people use in speaking with us rather than—which is what we normally do—reaching for their meaning and dropping the words, forgetting them. As we shall soon find, mental activity in the case particularly of reading is based to a very small degree on memory. Instead, in teaching reading, we shall be successful if we design our exercises and challenges in such a way that they can be integrated into the already mastered activities of the viewers and so are at once meaningful and made to work because of all the supporting equipment that each viewer brings with him when he yields to the impact of the program.

We shall be successful because we shall have removed our preconceptions from his way and rather than imposing on him our determination that he read, we shall have asked the question: What must we present to his discriminating mind that will make him say —"I now have another system of signs and rules that up to a point is isomorphic to a system I already own for understanding and speaking my mother tongue."? —or, "By observing the rules and using this system of signs, I am using only an alternative to the system of sounds I know so well how to use when I want to express myself and reach others for communication."? In putting our task this way, we shall be successful because for talkers and speakers, reading offers indeed a very small challenge, which cannot take long to master.

In developing the following programs, we have assumed the presence of an adult sitting with the young people watching the programs.

The discussion of the programs necessarily must deal with details of a relatively specialized nature—the precise methods of teaching a particular skill—and so likely will be of most immediate interest to educators and programers. Other readers may wish to turn to the commentary on the first five lessons below.

THE METHOD.   On the screen (as we saw), it is possible to animate designs that can be associated with specific sounds (from the language spoken by the voices on the sound track). This animation is in effect an algebra, a mathematical system that not only sums up all the operations needed for the purpose we have in mind but without any doubt conveys to viewers what could take a long time to explain, and then with no guarantee of eliminating the confusion that follows the use of words.

Hence basic to this teaching of reading is the presentation of examples of this sort of algebra, using

73

the few signs (to each of which one sound corresponds at the outset) that provide a considerable yield and encourage the viewers' acceptance of a method of working with words that will increase in importance and significance as we go along.

FIRST LESSON. As soon as one sign (e.g. a letter) has been put on the screen and a sound (in this case, of the English language) associated with it, it becomes possible to show that some transformations of the sign *do not* affect this relationship. If the sign is magnified or reduced in size, the voice still makes the same sound. A few moments spent on this exercise will create the certainty that whenever we see this sign, a given sound can be uttered with it.

On the screen it is now possible to show this sign, to take it away, and at intervals of time selected by the programer to show it again, in each instance of its presence repeating its sound. This device utilizes the succession of emissions of the same sound, hence it points to the time between utterances. When the succession is as short as could be, i.e., when the blended sounds are still distinguishable, a new sign, showing two of the previous signs horizontally contiguous, appears on the screen. The voice makes twice this sound as a blended sound. We therefore have a new sign with a new sound but a sound that has been generated from one already practiced.

We now can play a number of games with our signs:

– On the screen at its center appears the first or the second sign, then one or the other appears again, the sequence continually alternating so that it is not possible to guess which will appear.

– Now we can start a little on the left and draw one of the two signs and leave a little time before either the same or the other appears on its right—and on the right of this another, and so on. Because of this pause, we are forcing the viewer to place an inner bet with himself before the sign on the right appears, and we generate in him the true state which recognizes: "Until I see it, I cannot say which it will be for certain."

— We thus also have generated on a horizontal line from left to right, leaving small equal spaces between the signs, a "sentence" in the "language" of these two sounds. We now have the possibility of conveying the idea that with only two signs and two sounds we can form any number of "sentences" through the ordinary algebra of combinations and permutations of these combinations and permutations.

To make this easily comprehensible, we shall give our signs names.* If the first sign is *a* and its sound the sound at the beginning of *at*, the second sign is *aa*, and examples of "sentences" are:

```
a a a a
aa aa aa
a aa
aa a
a aa a aa aa a
```

And so on.

It is clear that this game will give to viewers a set of rules that is part of the activity of reading, that the rules will have not been taught but rather will have been practiced and applied with understanding—and that the medium of television can take care of everything involved so far.

SECOND LESSON. It is clear now that the viewers who could make the sound for *a* can *read* any text in the language that uses only the "words" *a* and *aa*. Had we

---

* *We have left unnamed the original sign and the corresponding sound so as to leave readers free to choose their own designations for them. Our own choice has nothing miraculous about it and comes from the experience of having developed reading schemes in Romance languages.*

chosen instead *i* as in *it, e* as in *pet, o* as in *top,* or *u* as in *up,* the lesson would have been essentially as easy.*

Hence for our second lesson we shall *transfer* the acquired knowledge of the rules to these other four vowels. This we do through two procedures with different rhythms. At first we introduce *u* as if it were the first vowel met, but at a much faster pace than with *a* in the first lesson. This reduction in time proves that transfer has taken place. Then we introduce a language of the two sounds and two signs of *a* and *u*. Here something new makes its appearance. The sequence *a, u,* forming one word *au,* sounds very differently than the sequence in the word *ua.* The two words are *reversals* one of the other. They can be animated on the screen by having *a* appear first and then putting a *u* at one corner on the screen and making it run towards *a.* The *u* can first place itself level on the left, leave *a,* and run to the right, and do this once or twice to draw attention to the order on the line from left to right. The voice would sound these words as they are formed. Next, sentences can be formed from these words.

Then we introduce the language of *i* as we did *a* and *u,* followed by a scene in which *a* and *u* are on the screen and *i* appears at a corner and runs to form *ia* and *ai,* then *iu* and *ui,* after which the three run towards each other forming the six permutations: *aiu, aui, uai, uia, iau, iua.* Sentences follow using these three sounds, to make it clear that the rules for reading sentences remains the same as in lesson one except

---

* *That we need to choose a vowel is obvious. That we need to choose one of the vowels just listed will be obvious if we listen to our voice when we say the vowels in the words* ate, fine, home, use. *These vowels in reality are diphthongs since two sounds are involved in their articulation. The choices left of one-sound vowels appear in such words as* police, father, put *or* to. *We therefore have good reasons to begin our exercises with the ones above and to leave diphthongs (known as long vowels by inattentive teachers) and sounds that are less frequently met for later study.*

that now we have three signs and three sounds to play
with and that the order of sound in words matter in
order to distinguish permutations. The lesson ends
after *e* and *o* have been introduced the same way.

Though it has not been necessary to call attention
to the fact up to this stage, we will, when introducing
the vowels, use on color television different colors for
the five vowels. We do it so as:

— not to name the sign but still give a clue for it,

— to give two clues where one may be sufficient
and thus assist those who are not color-blind (95 per-
cent of the population) who, when evoking a sound,
can think of a color,

— to prepare the ground for the demands of spell-
ing, which in some languages are many, but the discussion of which would take us too far afield. (The color
clue gives physiognomy to words and helps in retaining the sound to be made for them.)

On black and white television sets, various shadings of
grey will be used to distinguish the five vowels. In
presenting the succeeding lessons, we shall assume the
availability of color.

THIRD LESSON. There will be no need for reviewing the
work done before because it was so simple, so logical,
and so well practiced. But because we are unfolding
the language, each lesson, in adding its new material,
will bring back to it what is relevant from the previous
lessons.

The screen now shows the five isolated vowels in
any location the designer chooses. A brown sign having the shape *p* appears but no sound is heard. This is
because *p* is a consonant, the first we introduce, and
con-sonants only sound with. *p* runs and places itself
level before one of the vowels—say, *i*—and the voice
says "pi," as in *pin*. Then *p* jumps to the other side,
forming *ip* and "ip" is heard, as in *tip*. The jump back

and forward is done twice more, once with the sounds heard, once with the sounds left to the viewers. Then *p* runs to another vowel—say, *a*—to form, in whatever order, *pa* and *ap*, both of which are sounded when formed. Then the five vowels form a ring around *p* at the center. *p* is now animated so as to feign going to a vowel that fidgets as if inviting *p* to pair up with it.

This game would keep viewers alert and simultaneously would provide ten dfferent syllables distinguishable either by the composition or the order of the signs in the words.

Then nine more brown letters *p*, identical with the first, come in to form the ten pairs:

ap, pa, up, pu, ip, pi, ep, pe, op, po

Each (in any order) is lit up for a little while to give more chances to viewers to secure their grasp of the ten syllables.*

Then the syllables change their place so that *pa* faces the other nine syllables—*ap, pi, ip, pu, up, po, op, pe, ep*. As *pa* comes closer to *ap*, the two syllables are sounded with a shorter and shorter silence between them until, when the *a* of *pa* and the *a* of *ap* cover each other and *pap* is shown, the sound "pap" is heard.

Likewise *pu* and *up* become *pup; pi* and *ip, pip; pe* and *ep, pep; po* and *op, pop.***

Here we would have a chance to test our teaching by not sounding all or some of these latter four new words, so as to give a chance to our viewers to contribute, through their understanding of the game, their own estimate of what they know are the sounds

---

* *Indeed the number ten is only descriptive. There are two rules of formation, one in which one vowel is substituted for another (already practiced in the second lesson) and the reversal of words (met a number of times so far).*
** *All the two syllable words belong to the English language but do not need to be considered as such in this context.*

of the words. It should be understood that our statements about what children do in front of a television set when watching, has been supported by the author's investigations.

If the test proves that viewers are not baffled by what we are proposing and do produce the traditional sounds, we would have gained much more than the time saved by leaving the exercise to them. We would have learned something about children learning to read.

If the test proves that we have trusted children beyond what other teachers would consider reasonable and that there is need for more assistance in sounding the five words formed, we will have to postpone only until the next lesson the granting of independence to viewers.

FOURTH LESSON. In this lesson the first half of the scenario is very much like that of lesson three. This time a magenta sign *t* appears and dances like the brown sign *p* did, until we end with the appearance of the words *tat, tut, tit, tet, tot* of which the fourth is not part of the English language.

The second part of this lesson is also animated. At the top of the screen appear the five vowels, below them the two consonants *p* and *t*. Each of these signs will "secrete," in the order determined by the programer, a double that runs toward another to form pairs consisting of a vowel and a consonant (*up, at, it,* and so forth). Then "triples" are formed—first there appears the ten listed above (*pap . . . pop, tat . . . tot*), then a syllable with *p* (*pa*) and a syllable with *t* (*at*) merge to produce *pat*.

Now *t* and *p* rotate—as in the lesson given in note 12 of this chapter—to form alternately *tap* and *pat*. Elsewhere, and at the same time, *ta* and *ap* run towards each other to form *tap*. As *t* and *p* rotate around *a*, the word *tap*, when formed, "looks" at *pat*, "waits" a moment until it is formed again, and "rushes" to merge with it. After going through a new rotation, it becomes *pat*. Now a double is secreted and moves away and, while it does this, the rotation of its consonants produces *tap*, to which *pat* "comes" closer, as if to reconnoiter it, but "leaves" alone until the word, through rotation, once again becomes *pat*.

pit and *tip*, *top* and *pot* are studied likewise so as to force viewers to look carefully at similar words before coming to a conclusion on how they sound. In this manner, the new words are formed: *pat, tap, pit, tip, top, pot, pet*. Now the screen is filled with all the combinations obtained so far.* The lesson ends by lighting each in turn, but in a random order.

FIFTH LESSON. Having established visually by these devices the rules of the game of forming and merging syllables, we can in this lesson do two jobs.

One consists of introducing, in two different corners of the screen, two *s* signs, one green and one purple. The green runs rapidly towards the vowels— which appeared on the screen from the start as in the previous lessons—jumping in front of each to form the syllables *sa, su, si, se, so*, whose doubles fall under the vowels. These syllables are not sounded. Meanwhile the purple slowly and hesitatingly mingles on the right only with *a* and *i* to form *as* and *is*. These two syllables are sounded as they are formed. Now *sa* in a jump forms *as* and is sounded ("ass"), *su* forms *us* and is sounded, etc. The rotation of the green, in addition to the color itself and the sound, will distinguish the new words dynamically from the two formed by the purple *s*.

The screen is now cleared of all writing.

For the second job, at the four corners of the screen there appears in quick succession each of the four consonants to show that they are of equivalent importance. One choice could be green (*s*) and brown (*p*) for the top corners, magenta (*t*) and purple (*s*) for the bottom.

---

* *Since* put *to be an English word uses another sound for* u *we do not show it.* tep *is not shown because it is not an English word.*

a appears from somewhere and runs to the purple, which secretes a double that forms *as* which runs to the central area of the screen. From the *a* of *as* a double is secreted that runs to the magenta to form *at*, which then moves towards the central area. Likewise from *i*, which now appears, *is* and *it* are formed. *u* forms *up* and *us*. *o* appears and now doubles from both *t* and *p* go to meet it, and a pas de deux precedes the formation of the two words *top* and *pot*. When *e* appears, three signs, the green, the magenta, and the brown, rush to join with it. The first to succeed in forming a word are the green and magenta, giving *set*. The brown, in a sad mood, returns slowly to its original position when all of a sudden the green of *set* runs towards it, brings it back to take the place the green itself had, thus forming *pet*, and the green goes to the other end of this word and forms *pets*.

The green, full of its discovery, leaves *pet*, hovers, and suddenly seems aware that it can go to *pot* to form *pots*, to *top* to form *tops*, and to *tap* and *pat* to do the same thing. Looking around, the excited green decides to put itself now on the left of words and forms *stop*, *spot*, *spat*, *spit*. But when going to the other words—to *pet*, for example—after joining them, leaves them as if having committed a sin.

Now a shower of green *s* is produced from the corner in which this sign first appeared, and while some signs run towards other words to form the above words, the three-sign words form doubles that join with one *s*. The screen is now full of words with *s*. A late *s* finding all places taken at the beginning of the words puts itself at the end of *stop* to form *stops*, leaves it to go to *spot* to form *spots*. At that moment, ten new *s* come quickly from the corner to form *sits*, *sets*, *pets*, and *stops*, *pats*, *pots*, *pits*, *taps*, *tips*, *tops*. These secrete the double of the word they were before the *s* joined them.

At the top of the screen the vowels have disappeared, and the twenty-nine words formed thus far are rearranged in a cascade:

as	is	at	it	up	us	
pat	tap	pit	tip	pot	top	
sat	sit	sits	set	sets	pet	
pats	taps	pits	tips	pots	tops	pets
spot	spots	stop	stops			

pets is lighted up, shakes, and produces its reverse *step*. As soon as this word is formed, a green *s* comes from the corner and runs to turn it into *steps*. The double of *step* frees itself from *steps*, shakes, and becomes *pets*. We now have thirty-one words, many containing the green *s*, only two containing the purple *s*.

To end the lesson, various words are lit in turn, to be sounded or not according to the results of testing, to form at different speeds the following patterns:

it			is		pat		
it	is	pat			it	is	pat

until the three sound like the statement—*it is pat*

is			it		pat		
is	it	pat			is	it	pat

until the three sound like the question—*is it pat*

is		pat		up		
is	pat	up		is	pat	up

until the three sound like the question—*is pat up*

sit		up		pat		
sit	up	pat		sit	up	pat

until the three sound like the order—*sit up pat*

pat		stops		at		stops
pat	stops	at	stops	pat stops at stops		

until the four sound like the statement—*pat stops at stops*

The screen is now divided vertically in two parts. Lighted words run to form the compact alignment that we usually use when writing, creating a few examples of sentences arranged from top to bottom and left to right of words written to trigger the sounds that sound strangely like English.

COMMENTARY ON THE FIRST FIVE LESSONS. Readers, I hope, will agree that we have used both the medium and what viewers bring with them, and that we can reach in five lessons a high level of competence in reading, an achievement that results only from the fact that we treated every rule, every notation, every suggestion in terms of imagery, true mental dynamics, and inner criteria. Our learners have contributed everything they could. We never took their place. There has not been any need for repetition as a way of learning because the material was restricted and was met naturally again and again.

Our viewers, who have watched and played the games by supplying the sounds for the signs and the exercises shown, can be said to be reading—even, to be reading fluently. They comprehend the meaning of the sounds they make because their intonation supplies the meaning of the spoken mother tongue, which they have been able to use at the level we demanded of them since they were three or thereabouts.

The only valid objection to such a treatment of reading—and it should be clear that any other objection is beside the point—would be the fact that I have failed to prove here that this way of working is indeed akin to the functioning of the mind of viewers of preschool age.

If these five lessons were to be filmed and tried out in a number of nursery school classes or homes, according to our instructions, and if they were successful, further lessons can be filmed and tested so as to complete the teaching of reading to preschool children by television in perhaps twenty lessons.

19. *Summary of the Next Few Lessons.* In the first five lessons, we examined nine sounds and the eight signs on which they were based. We now have to extend the field. How to introduce new material is the challenge in front of us. In the case of the English language, the challenge can best be met by proceeding from a study of the nine sounds we have selected to

all the sounds of this language, then to all the spellings (or signs).

All the sounds need to be known by the programers. There are fifty-one. Twenty-one we classify as vowels because they have a sound of their own. The balance consists of thirty consonants, which only sound when joined to a vowel to form a syllable. But in English there are about three hundred different forms for these fifty-one sounds. (See Appendix C.)

It is now simply a matter of organizing the material so as to move out systematically from what has been conquered to a larger area.

Each successive lesson will embrace larger tasks. This can be done precisely because each step will make the learners more competent. Each lesson does not in a sense meet the same viewers, for after each lesson each viewer changes to the extent that he integrates what was offered him in the lesson. What these lessons present is not knowledge as quantity, something to be cut into slices of certain thicknesses so as to be assimilated in given time periods. Rather, they offer a quality of the mind, a way of knowing that attacks a series of tasks of certain increasing levels of difficulty, the materials being presented so that one is equipped to tackle each lesson in turn. This way of working equips learners to do every time more than they have done the day before.

The next few lessons are outlined in Appendix B. But even on the basis of what already has been developed, we make two claims.

First, that the above techniques make reading a meaningful exercise for preschool viewers, who will acquire this skill as a by-product of the mental exercises that form the games to be played with the signs and sounds. Second, that the cumulative effect of learning would permit viewers to meet and probably master the whole set of signs of the English language in a few weeks of viewings at the rate of half an hour per day.

4.

What About Other Ages?

The concentration on preschool children in the previous sections was motivated by the current public interest in using television to educate such children in the home. Since the possibility of doing this is conceived as a special opportunity for television, many minds have been at work on how the medium might serve this captive audience.

Still, television and its audience present other opportunities to be used profitably by educators of various age groups. These opportunities we shall discuss briefly in this section of the book, to indicate that we are aware of their existence and that the approach taken in this book has something to offer the whole range of age groups.

1. Children of school age watch television and have favorite programs; there are also programs that do not attract them at all.

Let us subdivide this large group of children from five to eighteen, into at least three subgroups, using for the basis of this division what the children are trying to make sense of spontaneously and not according to what they do at school.

In the first group, we shall put all those who are using their whole self so as to master the many workings of their various systems, actually and potentially.

In the second group, we shall put those who, having mastered their place in the universe of expression resulting from the integration of perception and action, enter the world of power and find themselves giving reality to what was transcendental so far. Their body is made to grow rapidly, their self-consciousness throws them back upon themselves, they discover the realm of conscious feeling, elect their first real friend or friends (very few of them), are invaded by the mystery of the self, know themselves as lived and in contact with what overwhelms them; they are cut off from the "logic of things" and are not yet in the logic of their culture, which remains transcendental. Their capacity to relate becomes a burden and they question everyone and find that liking and loving are much more complicated than ever before. Their sex, as one of the more easily expressed concomitants of how to relate, occupies more of their attention. They investigate sexuality in so far as it can become a part of the self that one can project and one can use objectively to express power and its dynamics.

In the third group, we shall put those who, having explored the ways of expressing power, want to take one of them to some extreme, asserting by this their entry into a world they have only felt around them and suffered from and looked at without much understanding, which may have led to fear, resentment, envy, irresistible pull, etc.

If it is the field of the intellect that they want to take to an extreme, they become conscious of the powers of thinking, of the organization of knowledge in the fields of the sciences, literature, history, and become very quickly a well of science, having stored huge amounts of scholastic knowledge ready to come out at the slightest call.

If they commit themselves to the field of love, they adhere to ideals with such resolution that they

try the paths of devotion and dedication with no second thought. It is when they direct themselves to this
field that they give themselves to a religious order, to
a movement of youth based upon such lofty ends as
liberation, nationhood, charity, or help.

If it is the field of physical excellence, their body
has grown enough to guarantee innerly that energy is
available and the will is in control of its economy, and
they become the devotee of games and sports to the
point of giving up comfort and other gifts, which they
know to exist and which have been important in the
previous stages of their living.

Behind all these words, readers must see that it is
possible to consider growth as directed from the center
of the self and differences between individuals as the
result of the choices permitted by life. Because we do
not look at life here as a genetic potential routinely
unfolding in conformity with the constraints of the
environment, we can see each person as a unique being
who has pursued one of the many lives open to each
and who is capable of entering into and coming out of
paths under the push of the will in conjunction with
the results of how the will meets the pressures of
other wills.

2. The quick classification above indicates that we
can use television to present these age groups with
selective programs that will assist them in their growth.
Some of the programs will cater specifically to the
needs that separate one group from another, while
other programs will serve to bridge particular areas
that range across all the groups. Indeed the characteristic of growth being both total involvement in what
must be mastered before one can move ahead and then
transcendence of the activities, once the mastery is
achieved we have to separate and unify in turn.

As to the results, it is obvious that the appeal of
the programs serving the aspect of total involvement
will be greater for those viewers who are at that particular stage in their exploration of life, than it will be

for those who have not yet the need to be there or for those who have already lived through it. Even so, the latter may still be deeply absorbed in what is presented, for the shows may present them with challenges not met earlier in their own explorations. The former may look and not understand or be bored and turn away.

Since the rotation of the earth and the birth of new children fill the world with people variously going through life more or less needing to encounter experiences that in comparable ways permit them to make their gifts explicit and to make sense of *their* world, we shall have to offer programs that are valuable for each of the age groups defined above plus the other three age groups that, with preschoolers, exhaust the full range of growth—pre-adults, adults, and senior citizens.

3. Let us call pre-adults all those who are today still unable to transcend society and adults those who today are manipulating society for their own ends or ideals. Senior citizens are those who are not any longer permitted by life to call themselves adults in the above sense.

Here again age is not the criterion but rather what one has done and is doing with oneself. People of any age who believe that society is an all-powerful entity are pre-adults, while people of any age who can force change upon the behavior of some group endowed with social power are adults. Many examples of both come at once to mind.

Adults are the people who have least need for special programs on television because they live in society, mold it, are themselves in the news, and have little time for viewing.

Pre-adults are already catered for by the overwhelmingly social programs that constitute the analyses of life around them and which form the bulk of today's shows. That these programs can vastly be improved is well known and is the job of critics already at work on behalf of this group.

Networks are highly sensitive to adults and pre-adults because they are the bread earners of the country and those who keep its businesses going. To meet their needs, when they are expressed, will be no problem. The goodwill of those running the stations is extended to them in a way it is given neither to senior citizens nor to children and adolescents. This is why new proposals for these last groups are needed. The programs will be acceptable to all and therefore shown on television if they make these viewers conscious of their needs and make business conscious of how to satisfy these needs at a profit.

What About Other Ages?

4. *Programs for Children of School Age.* Here we shall only outline our suggested programs.

CHILDREN. The group of young people who accept being called boy and girl and are not worried that they are small and not too strong, will be the targets of our first group of programs.

These children are engaged essentially in making sense of the workings of everything in the universe. They are only slightly centered on emotions; they naturally feel less than they will at the following period and will endure much more physical pain (if it is related to their investigations) than they will later. They concentrate upon reaching a level of excellence in a number of directions, ignoring others altogether. They want in particular to make each set of muscles be under the immediate call of their will, to perform actions that become ever more complicated. What inspires them is to engage in activities that do not require words. They fathom such activities directly with their senses and are challenged by them to integrate their senses and their muscles so they can overcome new obstacles.

In order to achieve this mastery in "finesse," their body is not left to grow at the rate it experienced earlier in life and that will be resumed at the following stage. Boys and girls hold themselves at a manageable level, not too small to be prevented from taking certain steps, such as leapfrogging or skipping rope, nor so big that they need to be concerned with their own bulk.

While three to five year olds move and run, use tricycles with *maestria*, they are far less competent on roller skates, bicycles or ice skates which for the next age form tremendous attractions. In fact this age (seven to ten) is ideal for serving as apprentices in a large number of uses of oneself. It is therefore right that we should develop activities that will take such children far ahead on the road to their realization, for the children will accept them at once as meaningful and the activities will stretch their aptitudes beyond what chance offers everyone.

Already the scout movement (cubs), films like the series with Tarzan, have shown that what inspires this age is a mystique of action which hardens the individual, and organizes actions and perception within meaningful immediate ends—doing a good deed or saving a friend in the jungle. Kim and Lassie are inspiring figures because their environment is restricted, dangerous (because of the physical obstacles within it rather than for social reasons), and, in so far as one cannot guess what may come, mysterious—but is still not beyond the resources of a boy or a dog.

Indeed the imagination of this age and how it controls its universe both indicate where we shall find the source of programs to satisfy it and tell us how to treat the material within such programs.

As one principle to follow, we can see that *depth* is a good standard. Everything we shall attempt to present on the programs will move from a cursory encounter to a closer and closer examination of it.

The display of how life has provided animals with movement can fill programs showing in slow motion the relation of different pieces of the bodies of amoebae, worms, slugs, snails, reptiles, etc., to the surfaces on which they advance.

Another suitable subject is the various ways animals have of determining who is a friend or a foe, and how they respond to either. Already a number of pro- grams picture life in the jungle. These programs arouse interest. What is needed now is a systematic treatment of these subjects, at the level that shows all the ways available to animals to master an aspect of the universe of activity. The stress in the programs should no longer be on survival of the fittest but on the way—regardless of how one masters what is re- quired of one in the world—one can carry on a life of some sort that allows for the expression of one's gifts, and enables one to find a place in the world for such a set of behaviors. Such programs will make plain that there is room in the world for all sorts of behaviors and that man can comprehend them all and find them adequate for some sort of living.

The survival of the fittest should not be the only vision to explain the right to live of the beings that now exist on our planet. A proper examination of the evidence may serve to provide every viewer with a more complete and more adequate insight into the actual content of the world, and to open up each to new vistas.

When we have shown that so many ways of being exist and that in each "perfection" of behavior means to obey the laws of what can be done with what has been given one, it is possible to ask the question: what has been given man?

Obviously this provides the basis for another series of programs which can be linked to the previous ones or treated separately.

While their number is not large, there are enough men and women who have devoted part of their lives to mastering some skill that most of us only dream of or at a certain moment in life suspect exists, but leave untouched.

Television would be an excellent means of dem- onstrating for this age group the type of exercises that, when practiced, would yield comparable sorts of competence. Presenting the best uses of oneself that

living mankind can offer so as to nourish the spontaneous involvement of this age group in the use of
oneself as a dynamic system, may lead our humanity
to a conception of education much more significant
than the deadening intellectually insignificant exercises
of today. Television will justify the expenses, required
by the subject matter, of filming the masters of balance, of the jump, of the synchronization of movements, by showing to millions of youngsters what can
be done with one's body before it becomes fixed in
its ways. Precisely because it is possible for television
to open up a world of activity to children of this age,
enabling them to integrate both what they can comprehend at once because their consciousness dwells in
it and what represents the conquered frontiers in the
realm of action, we may find that it has been really
inexpensive, per capita, to educate our young generation in the true mastery of the soma. The end, sheer
delight in the total use of one's potential.

Besides man and animals, this age is interested in
the workings of machines.

There are so many of them and so many principles
at play in them that a display of machines will furnish
each mind with an enormous supply of visual equipment with which to examine the causes of various
machine breakdowns. No viewer will have to memo-
rize, or label pieces in isolation; each viewer will
realize a dynamically integrated system that can in
turn be integrated to form bigger systems with increased effectiveness and bigger ranges.

Levers and their transformations (pulley, shafts,
cranes . . .), cogged wheels and their associations (in
watches, differentials . . .), pumps and their variations
(inflators, compressors, suckers, rarefiers, vacuum
pumps . . .), and combinations in rotors, engines, etc.,
are all attractive to anyone concerned with the sub-
tleties of action and a survey of how mankind has
conquered the realm of mechanics.

To cover all this, years of filming and of showing
will be needed, but we shall have given this age group

what is relevant to its life, to the concerns it is working on spontaneously and thoroughly—by means of the
fact that television is in every home and can be pro-
gramed for millions with one expense.

The education of this age group will not end with
the contact of each of its members with television.
Schools, travel, homes, and the immediate environment will add their shares—unique, direct, personalized,
differing by virtue of the differences of those who
contribute to the education and the spot where it is
lived.

ADOLESCENTS. Precisely because the world is not only
activity and perception, precisely because man is also
socialized in tribes, families, neighborhoods, etc., there
are other dimensions to being. Adolescence is the time
of our life when, assured of having made sense of the
environment, its variety and challenges, and of having
developed the means to deal with it, we turn towards
ourselves to see the human in ourselves and in others.

Seen in this perspective, adolescence demands programs that complement its spontaneous study of our
affectivity at work.

There is no end to what we can offer. Novels in
great numbers have been written, are being written,
and will be written to tell about the singularities of
man in the various degrees of his involvement with
his human environment.

We therefore already have guidelines for our programs. Adolescents live intensely within the moving
world of their emotions and of their feelings. They
enter wholeheartedly into their experiences which, to
begin with, mainly involve their own self, then expand
to include one more person (the beloved friend), then
the beloved one of the other sex or God or both.

The self gaining sight of its immenseness, feels
awe and looks for one who can share this vision. Parents won't serve because they are engaged in what
makes sense to them, not in what makes sense to their
troubled children discovering their powers. Power,

this is what characterizes the adolescent. Not social power, but raw power which manifests itself in the growing body, the growing powers of love and thought which now permit one to replace finesse by sheer quantity. How the adolescent can stand pain, love, treachery, jealousy, solitary expression of misery, eroticism, arrogance, virtual conquests, gazing at oneself in complacency, etc.! He rejects everything for no visible reason, just as he accepts anything for no better reason. Society is no longer a frame, it contains obstacles, puts on him demands he has not felt even if earlier he had noticed and ignored them. Morality in him is awakened because he is confused and looks for lights in the environment, the whole of which is going on as before. He is unconscious that he needs such lights, and makes no attempt to provide them—until clashes occur between the adolescent and the environment.

If novels to illustrate all the inner movements of the confused seeker do not exist, television programers and writers have a world to explore to develop the art of animating conflicts that result in enlightenment.

The Romantic movement of about two hundred years ago is similar, at the level of adult life, to this search for the meaning of the soul seeking to know itself. What an opportunity for the magnifying glass of the writers who are fascinated by the fluidity of all this inner life of millions of people left undernourished by an adult society wholly immersed in its own search for significance. What an opportunity for television to present in its striking and true medium, examples of the searches in depth that have shaped each of us—more or less—in our time!

Adolescent viewers are seeking. They are seeking themselves as people who can function independently in the areas of strength, of love, and of the intellect. They are equipped for these tasks with much of their past, which to them now seems useless: earlier they were naturally egocentric and now they look for a companion; earlier they were naturally engaged in satisfying their quest for understanding the fit and relationship between details, now they are overwhelmed with powerful insights that do not for long remain the same and continually present them with alternatives that are rarely decisive. They cannot make sense of what they perceive for the first time, which they do not see in its entirety. Every one of their former impressions gains new dimensions and new significance. Each becomes troublesome and throws the adolescent into a field of questions that cannot be asked—for he does not yet have words—and cannot be answered, since no one knows of the questions or seems interested in knowing them.

This adolescent needs to satisfy himself that he is not peculiar, that if he is discovering a world that is not the one his parents occupy or imagine, that someone else is confronting the same world too. His search for a true friend almost always succeeds. Together they comfort each other, let each other know that such behaviors as theirs are in the line of nature, not of the insane. The sweetness of this new kind of companionship gives the word friend a meaning it never had. Now another is present in one's feelings. When the friends meet, they find they have not parted.

Activity no longer punctuates the adolescent's passage of time, broken by hiatuses, as in childhood. Now, there is consciousness of continual living, of the flowing of time, which is concretized by felt thoughts, loaded images, and by endless dialogues involving two people experiencing their world. Earlier comparable dialogues involved the self and the universe of things. The "logic of things" is no longer binding. The reigning logic is like some fluid stuff that soon can look differently from how it now seems. The possibility or existence of contradiction is not yet a compelling reason for the adolescent to suspend his judgment. Since his self is always at work pouring new material into the arena of his consciousness, the adolescent knows that what he just has stated is not all he could say, hence he does not allow anyone to hold him to his words. The adolescent does his thinking when he is alone, not when he talks at random. His image as an intellect is based on what is actually a genuine *feeling* of thinking, and is a response to the impact of the ideas that move in him and gain expression. If ever speech is for expression and not for communication, it is during this searching period when the greatest weight is given to what goes on within rather than to whatever it is that the listener is hearing. But expression is taking place, and those who know how to listen to a seeking person can discover by their own efforts what is being communicated as well.

All this is beautiful stuff for programs that must seek to display the same kind of logic in situations that can so easily be made fluid on screens, expressing that which is constantly unfinished but is always being worked on.

Whether stories are serialized, or single items are selected for illustration, any programer with the capacity to feel like an adolescent will have no difficulty in transmuting into a telling show his insight into a soul in the making, and thus leave viewers filled with a new understanding and perhaps even the suspicion that the real person we fail to see in every adolescent is genuinely trying to make sense of all those gifts that suddenly have been bestowed on him.

POST-ADOLESCENTS. This is the group that has done what life permitted and who now no longer considers the turmoils of the inner self as the most important arena of life. They want a place in the sun. They want to be acknowledged socially. But the society into which they are emerging has a history, has been molded by actions and thoughts and attitudes of people they cannot meet and know. They must make sense now, and persistently, of so many components of their social environment that it is absurd for one to ask them what they think and believe. None of their social concepts has been sufficiently studied by them, for them to be able to be intellectually responsible for it.

The programs for this age will need rethinking. Post-adolescents are in need of experience in the large. They cannot conceive of what society offers them because modern societies are so complex and are the outcome of historical pressures which they cannot perceive fully but feel must have some impact upon their own lives.

So one line of approach to programs could be to dramatize biographies of men and women who have spent years and years in understanding what it is to be a skilled, responsible, complete occupier of a social position. Such dramatization does not mean fanciful treatment of idiosyncrasies in order to make a "good drama." On the contrary, it means taking the true life of a person whose daily acts portray real opportunities in society and show the demands that society puts to its members before it recompenses them for their contribution. Truth about the detailed working of society in its various layers and places—this is what will inform the post-adolescent about society, as life up to this point has informed him about the world of action and things and the world of feeling.

Society has used the lever of inspiration when dramatizing the biographies of "great men." This type of biography is already available, is valid for the few who attain eminence in their nations. But for the typical viewer, the viewer who is everyman, our proposal will fill a gap in the availability of data that in fact exists hidden in our societies and needs to become as much a part of the fabric of everyone's life as sunsets or melodies.

We may seem to be extremely utilitarian in our proposals and may seem not to leave a sufficient place for the arts on television.

This book is written in the hope that something new can be added to the role of television in education. Art, and the arts, are involved at every stage in every one of our proposals. We do not need to state explicitly that concerts, exhibitions, the showing of distinguished artists and craftsmen at work, can all help in the education of viewers. Indeed, it should be clear that if all the ideas in this book are to be implemented and become programs, the progress achieved by television as a medium will be such that the thinking expressed here will appear as shallow and short-sighted. In a way, such an outcome is the best thing a writer of a book like this can expect for his work.

5. *Programs for the Last Three Groups.* Since adults are defined here as the people who are responsible for the changes in society, it will be their responsibility to give themselves the programs they need to make sense of where they are going and what they are doing with themselves, with others, and for others.

Still, because the members of these three groups have finished or are finishing their formal education, most of them will have acquired ways of thinking that mainly are reflections of the cultures of the past. They might not be able to discover easily what a visual culture could be and could do for them. On a number of occasions, they are likely to be caught between a world functioning in ways to which they have not been introduced and one functioning in the ways they were forced to acquire when they were not those who decided what to do with people.

The following proposal is but one of those that could be made to serve all three of these groups, whose members, in so far as their modes of thought are concerned, are in serious need of re-education.

What we usually do when we think via the medium of memorized words, which form so much of our verbal education, is to generate a static universe. Many of the transformations that underlie the acquisition of languages are beaten out of our consciousness, and we are made to believe primarily in the existence of individual objects without much link between them, our perceptions culminating in an atomized universe whose meaning remains beyond our reach. Our critical powers are not developed in the direction of questioning evidence, of looking for whatever is needed to make sense of anything. We are made dependent on those among ourselves who are thinkers, and we look to them for solutions.

To bring a change in this situation we must re-educate adults so as to make them trust their perception more than they trust other people's words; and help them to acquire a dynamic imagery that permits them to scan a world of possibilities contained in situations that involve variables; and enable them to learn, by working on new problems that have not been part of their education, that they are capable of developing mental tools no matter what their age—and then have them test these tools on meaningful challenges that are indicative of how the future will work.

One thing is becoming increasingly clear every day and this is that we have to develop a dialogue of informed people rather than put someone who knows in front of a person who does not know and let the one tell the other what he knows whether or not the second has any criteria to ascertain the truth of what he hears from the first.

Whenever we place two people in front of a situation they can look at, it is almost impossible to say who will see more and what significant things will be seen by which of them. Most of us are equal when it is a matter of looking and seeing, regardless of the fact that we might choose to stress some features of the situation rather than others.

Adults who functioned early in their childhood as "visuals" have been distorted by a verbal education and no longer know what it is to be a "visual."

Television, as they see it, is an extension of the radio. But it is not. Television forces us to receive an infinite number of items at once all the time we are viewing. We only need to remove the verbal side of the programs to force viewers to use their gifts of vision. We must seek to develop a complete visual code that feeds information without words and forces viewers to drop the habit of verbalization they currently need in order to feel that they understand a message.

Adults in the space age, the nuclear age, the computer age, are still functioning as their ancestors did in the Middle Ages. Verbalization is really valid only for the areas where words can trigger images that become the carriers of meaning. People who feel the necessity to verbalize can be confounded if they are requested to express what verbally is inexpressible, or even extremely complicated.

Facing the world of tomorrow with the new demands it will make, requires that we use our mental tools for what these tools do best. There is a place for words but not every place. There is a place for quick thinking, a place for thinking of wholes, and a place for awareness of the appropriate mental tools needed by situations.

Television can contribute to giving adults once more the use of their imagery, of a quick and complex way of thinking.

To achieve this we need a kind of film in which the components are so selected that they force ideas to emerge without the accompaniment of words and in such a way that, on the part of the viewers, no words have the time to form themselves.

Because we can get an impact through our eyes that does not need to be remembered and remains in us by the energy it adds to the mind in the form of an image that can be recalled at once and in terms of mental energy, we can now through television submit people to the impact of colors, shapes, and intensities of our choosing and be sure that these selections have affected them. This means that, for any future learning, we can count on this wealth being in their minds, and we can act upon its presence by means that at a very small cost in energy generate infinite classes of equivalences, whose operation is a basic mode of thought. In the process, the mind will enrich itself with:

— the infinities that it perceives in the transformations,

— the capacity to transform any image into another.

When this mode of thought becomes second nature, the viewers can act upon their own thinking,
looking for transformations compatible with attributes
of classes that they find in their mind.

Today we know enough about how to achieve
this to generate a large number of programs that will
give every adult what ignorance and preconceptions
have prevented him from acquiring during his education, a power to think quickly and correctly in a complex way on complex things.*

A final comment. While this book does not treat
the needs and interests particular to senior citizens, a
brief word about them is appropriate, precisely because its members have more time for viewing than
do bread earners. Perhaps senior citizens can find in
the programs for all other ages the nourishment they
need. Perhaps they will come to like this kind of food
and rather than fall back into childhood rise through
it as they discover that enough innocence is left in
them to start a new life from scratch. All of which is
possible.

---

* *Clearly we can use computers to aid us in utilizing this
power, as will be shown in a forthcoming monograph on
which the present writer has been working for some time.*

Conclusions
and Recommendations

Since this text was conceived of as an invitation to readers to discuss seriously how television can assist in the birth of a visual culture, it may be permitted the author to close the discussion with a monologue that summarizes his position.

Every one of the concrete proposals made in the last two chapters of this book being a testimony that ideas can be carried out to the point of realization, no one will doubt that the writer takes the view that it is his responsibility, and the responsibility of others in this area, to go beyond verbal discussion.

Because the several examples given in detail can be multiplied almost indefinitely, another dimension emerges. Such examples are evidence that the writer already has begun to live in a visual culture, already functions as a witness of the future, can meet at least in part the unfolding of demands different from those of the past in the realms of thinking, of research, of science, of social action.

Since this is possible for him, it follows that it is possible to all those who wish it for themselves. To all those wherever they are who will pioneer the new culture.

Because the education that is necessary for our time will be the creation of these witnesses, who will free the coming generation from the task of absorbing what it is not yet (but otherwise would become) committed to and which it need no longer bow to, education thus becomes the social and technical action that will permit the new man to emerge. To emerge conscious of what he can objectify in his life, recognizing in himself incomparably greater powers in his mind and finding more to explore in the universes that he unfolds by the process of living in them intensely and thoroughly.

What will give him this consciousness and make him into a man of the new culture is his awareness that understanding reality simultaneously involves the perception of the self in time and of what the mind is capable of noticing in the universe of which one is a part. No abrupt separation exists between an individual and the world around him, each gives reality to the other. Recognizing this, the new man would then know that every thought can be revised, that every impression is a stage in one's awareness, susceptible of change and of delivering up a new meaning.

The man of the new culture will know that the fabric of things is made of relationships that are never exhausted and when apprehended always betray the observer, as well as the observed, as being at a particular stage and moment.

The man of the new culture is ready to revise any and every one of his thoughts, ideas, attitudes, ideals, because he knows that his knowledge depends on his knowing and that this in turn depends on where he has taken himself on the road of perception. Because relativity is a universal attribute he has perceived in himself, in his knowing, and in what stands for his universe, he approaches every moment of life as one that is what it is, though he cannot say quite what.

To perceive a reality that changes in time is to perceive the real reality, not an unreliable set of illusions. The illusion is to believe in (and to believe one sees) an unchangeable or unchanging reality, for there is not a single example of such stability within or without.

The television set, once lit with its images, is a reminder of what we actually live in, a world in flux, an indefinitely renewable universe capable, once we become one with an image by surrendering ourselves to it, of generating a constant renewal of consciousness by acting on the sensitive springs within the viewer.

We now have the facility of knowing our self as time and to live its transformation into experience. Mastering the economy of the transformation of time into experience is one of the main jobs for the man of the new culture.

Looking at how we can educate through television, we find that we must see to it that as many people as possible recognize television for what it is. This is task number one.

When those who understand that television is a pre-eminent channel towards the visual culture are strong enough to be heard, they will display in their being the characteristics that will make them attractive, inspiring, and capable of generating change among others. Task number two is hence the formation of an elite of the new culture in the sense that some of those who know television for what it is find in themselves the means of expression that are conceived by others as a power worth possessing.

Task number three consists of the demonstration

— that those who are not yet committed to the values of the present cultures will not need much in order to become people of the new culture,

— that as people of the new culture they will function so much more easily in a much richer universe than their fathers did,

— that they will achieve returns for their thoughts and actions that are rarely realized at present.

From all this it will appear to all that the new culture is preferable to the previous ones.

The men of the new culture will remain uncommitted because the new culture, unlike previous ones, does not demand identification with one vision, one form, one static reality.

As to the people who, in the process of receiving their education, have been made to give up the consciousness of their own role in grasping reality, it may be task number four to re-educate them, as we suggested was possible in the previous chapter.

In the writing of this book, task number one has been the obvious aim. Still, tasks number three and four have been approached in passing, at the virtual level at least.

Whether we will be a handful or a multitude who can think together of what has happened to the world since the old cultures have adopted television for some of what it offers, we shall know soon enough.

Appendix A

A New Musical Notation for Television

1. Because notational systems attempt to put in visual terms what is accessible through the intellect and through senses other than sight, it is possible to conceive of a number of such systems—as is witnessed by the various numerical notations offered in history, the various ways of noting speech that have been accepted by mankind, and the various musical notations used over the centuries.

Here we will be concerned with a notation for music.

It is clear that music is in time; and that time, as the stuff of music, can be structured by the durations of sounds and by the beats and meters that provide the "stations" for the flow of consciousness. Specific musical effects, besides those created by the temporal factors that go to form rhythms, are obtained by varying both the amounts of energy allowed to reach the ear and the frequencies (or notes) and their harmonics.

A musical notation that took into account all these components still would not take into account the adaptability of music to individual musicians (instrumentalists or singers) and instruments. Therefore, one

notation is to be considered an improvement over another if it can make obvious what in the other is
reachable only through a special initiation, more or
less demanding.

The present stave notation used in music provides
a symbolism that is immediately meaningful only in that
higher notes are placed higher up on the stave; and it is
anti-symbolic in that the shortest notes are represented
by the most decorated signs. In addition, so many
other signs are used to convey information deemed
necessary for the correct appreciation of the intentions of the composers, that music reading has been
found hard even by many people who are musically
endowed.

The proposal made here for a new form of notation is not fully developed, but it is offered because
television provides an opportunity to correct certain
defects of the traditional system.

2. A straight line has been used as a space reflecting
properties of time at least since the time of Chuquet,
a predecessor of Descartes. Mechanics and physics use
this model all the time. A straight line is the basis of
the notation proposed here.

It is easy to conceive that a piece of music can be
represented, temporally speaking, by a succession of
intervals on a straight line, the lengths of the successive
segments reflecting the durations of the successive
notes and silences.

To indicate the energy carried by the notes, each
segment can become the base of a rectangle whose
height represents the relative energy associated with
the note duration.

Color can be used to indicate particular notes.
Taking a sequence of seven color frequencies (one in
each band of the rainbow) to represent seven successive notes, it is possible to offer an absolute and a relative solution to the problem of representing musical
sounds, particularly if—after determining the optical
frequencies that correspond to the acoustic frequen-

cies—we color the rectangles representing the notes with colors of these frequencies.

With such a notation system readers in one glance will see the stretch of durations, their intensities, and the qualities of a tune that are translated by the colors. The beats will be obvious, as will the silences (blanks). The pattern of the colors will convey a mood. The length of a segment will inspire for a song a duration of breathing, and a train of segments will mobilize a syncopation or a different use of oneself.

3. On a TV screen it is possible to generate a tune as an unfolding process in which a colored rectangle appears on a horizontal line—the duration of this segment being exactly the duration of the note that is to be sung or hummed or played on an instrument—followed by a succession of colored rectangles of various lengths, revealed in a similar manner, to represent the successive notes of the tune.

The following example given in its totality would be shown as a deployment from left to right and then line by line, going from top to bottom, of the succession of colored rectangles that comprise it. The numbers indicate the length of the rectangle, or the duration of the note; the colors give the value of the notes.

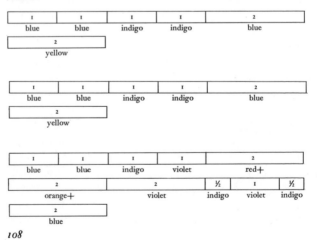

1	1	2	1	1
indigo	violet	red+	violet	indigo

4
blue

2	1	1	2½
indigo	blue	green	yellow

1½	1	1	1	1
green	blue	blue	red—	green

2	2
yellow	orange

4
red—

4
red—

4. Because the symbolism of this notation conveys so much by itself, it is easy to imagine a large number of uses of it in teaching music, vocal or instrumental, as well as in teaching about music. For instance, it is possible to act upon the perceptible variables in such a way as to make everyone aware of

   — the relation of breathing and the sustaining of notes (by letting the duration be stretched as long as one wants),

   — the character of a register and of the notes within or outside one's register (by stressing the ease with which the first group of notes are emitted and the impossibility of producing the others),

   — the difference between beat and rhythm (by acting on the way the colored rectangles flow one from the other in their appearance),

   — the difference between "forte" and "piano" (by acting upon the amount of color in the rectangles or the width of the rectangles as against their length).

   In a forthcoming publication, the contents of this Appendix will be developed more fully, using a number of examples to illustrate a teaching of music that is an education of musical awareness.

Appendix B

The Basis for
Three More Reading Lessons

The signs presented in the fifth and last reading lesson discussed in the text are listed in the following table.

*Table 2 **

a	u	i	e	o
p	t	s	s	
	tt	ss	ss	
			's	

The sixth and seventh lessons will be devoted to the differences between Table 3 and Table 2.

Table 3

a	u	i	e	o	a
					u
p	t	s	s	m	n
	tt	ss	ss	mm	nn
		's	's		

---

* *Table 1 is a chart of fewer signs and sounds.*

The eighth lesson will be devoted to the differences between Table 4 and Table 3.

Table 4

a	u	i	e	o	a	I
					u	

p	t	s	s	m	n	f	f	d
	tt	ss	ss	mm	nn	ff		dd
		's	's					

When we introduce new signs beyond Table 2, we do not need to go on doing the same work of animation we did in the first five lessons. Rather, we can use algebraic techniques.

Algebra is a school subject, but it also is the name of all the operations we all use when using our mind. To save ourselves time and maintain the fabric of what we already have learned, we integrate the new by finding its links with the old or recast the old so that it agrees with the new. To express this process, the operations of algebra are very helpful.

We have already met three such operations: reversals (which linked, for instance, *top* and *pot*), additions (which linked, say, *up* and *pup*), and substitutions (which linked, for example, *tip* and *tap*). If we add a fourth, insertions (which would link *pest* to *pet*, for instance), we would have as many operations as we need to introduce most sounds, as we shall now see.

In the sixth lesson, we let the orange sign *m* appear on the screen and have it meet *at* to form *mat*, which is sounded. *pat* (already known) appears and the *p* in it disappears as *m* takes its place—the sequence then is reversed and repeated—so that *mat* is obtained both by addition from *at* and by substitution from *pat*. *mat* then becomes *met*; *met* becomes *mess*; then *mess* becomes *miss*. *mess* or *miss* will produce first *moss* and then *mom* which in turn becomes *tom* and then *tim*. Each time a word appears, it is not necessarily sounded.

Then by insertion, *mat* becomes *mast,* and this becomes *must. mat* becomes *map* and this, by reversal,
pam which, reversed again, produces *map* which, by
substitution, yields *mop* and, by addition, *mops.*

pam becomes *sam* which becomes *mass* by reversal.

All these words can be crowded on the screen
with arrows in between. If we make the convention
that◄—r—►appears everytime we show a pair related
by reversal and◄···s···►appears everytime we use
substitution and—— a ——►whenever we add at either
end and ····i···►when we perform an insertion, the
screen using these words, will look like this:

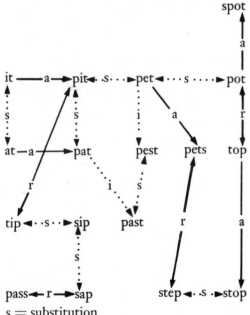

s = substitution
a = addition
r = reversal
i = insertion

Out of these and the previous words, we can generate a number of sentences which are as easy to read
as the words themselves.

— must pam sit up
— tom met mom at pam's
— pat's mast is up
— is it tom's

Next, two spellings for the schwa sound are introduced in a deep yellow color. This is done in two steps—first in the shape of *a* used at once in the following sentences

— it is a must
— pam is a pest

and then in the shape of *u* that will appear in the word *upon*. Then a lilac *n* is introduced by the syllables *in*, *an*, and *on*. Here too algebraic operations generate the words that use this sign and previous ones.

at	an	man	men	not	nut
in	pin	pen	ten	net	nuts
	pins	pens	tent		
spin	pun	sent			
	sun				
	sum	sums			

From these words come the sentences:

— ten men sat on a mat in a tent
— pam sent sam in
— it is not a man
— a nut spins on a map

These examples, all of which are presented in the sixth and seventh lessons, may suffice to prove that it is possible to move from one set of signs to a larger one and continue until the complete set of English signs is taken care of. Particular techniques will differ with the challenge at hand.

For this approach, the process of reading has been analyzed to the point that it can be presented through the medium of television as a procedure entirely under the control of programers and viewers.

Appendix C

The Signs and Sounds
of the English Language

The table on the next page contains all the signs and associated sounds of the English language. Each vertical column lists the different spellings used for a single sound. Put another way, all the spellings in a given column have the same sound. Thus, for example, the fifth column contains all the spellings for the sound of *o* as in *pot*:

oh   (as in John)
ho   (as in honor)
ow   (as in knowledge)
a   (as in swamp)

Column nine is the sound of *o* as in *more;* column thirteen the sound of *o* as in *go;* column sixteen the sound of *o* as in *do.*

Left side (vowel groups)

o   o
oi | oy
ee | ea | e | ie
oo | ou | u | ew | ui | o
o | oo | oe | ough | ou | u | ue | ui | ew | wo
a | ai | hei | ea | e | et | ayo

ou | hou | ow | ough
o | oe | ow | owe | oa | oh | ew | ou | eau | ough
e | ee | ea | ei | ie | i | eo | oe | ay | ey
u | you | eau | ue | ew | eu | eue | ieu

a | ay | ey | eigh | aigh | ei | ea | ai
o | a | au | aw | augh | ough | ou | oo | hau | oa
a | aa | ea | e | ah | au
i | y | i | igh | ie | eye | ye | eigh | is | ais
a | e | u | o | i | ea | ou | y | ei | ai | ough | ie | iou | io

o | oh | ho | ow | au | ou | a
e | ie | ea | ai | u | a
i | y | ey | u | o | ie | ia | a | ay | e | ai | ei | ui
u | o | oe | ou | oo
a

Right side (consonant groups)

x   x
x | xe | xc | cc
qu
j | g | d | dge | ge | gg | dg | di
ng | n
ch | tch | t | c
sh | ch | t | s | ce | che | ss | sch | sc | ci

g | gg | gu | gh | gue
h | wh
b | bb | be | bu
r | rr | re | rre | wr | rh | lo | rrh | t
k | kk | ke | ck | ch | c | lk | qu | que | cch | che | cc
w | wh | o | u
th | the

th | the
l | ll | le
d | dd | de | ed | ld
f | v | ve | ve | lve
f | ff | fe | ph | gh | u
n | nn | ne | kn | dne | pn | gn

m | mm | me | mb | gm | mn | lm
s | z | ge
s | ss | se | 's | c | ce | sw | st | sc | sch | ps
s | ss | se | z | zz | si | thes | x | 's
t | tt | te | ed | cht | ct | bt | pt | tte | th
p | pp | pe | ph

© C. Gattegno 1962

Dr. Caleb Gattegno for more than thirty years has been studying the dynamics of learning—the way teachers work on their students and the way students work on their subject matter—and out of his studies has developed a new body of techniques and materials. Much of his developmental work has concentrated on the areas of mathematics and reading. His method for teaching mathematics, which he calls "Numbers in Color"® and was based on the use of Cuisenaire rods, was developed in 1953; his method for teaching reading, "Words in Color," in 1957. Both are used in numerous countries (Words in Color has been developed for several major languages) and in areas throughout the United States.

Dr. Gattegno, born in Alexandria, Egypt, in 1911, has worked as an educator in many different capacities. From 1937 to 1945, he was director of the Institute of Higher Scientific Studies in Cairo. From 1945 to 1957 he was on the faculty first of Liverpool University (until 1946) and then of London University. After World War II, he was also instrumental in helping to renew interest in the work of Jean Piaget, two of whose books he translated. From 1957 to 1958, as a member of the Technical Assistance Board of the United Nations, he worked in Ethiopia, directing the preparation of new textbooks. Since 1966, he has been visiting the United States, continuing his activities through an organization he directs, Schools for the Future.

Dr. Gattegno's writings include: *Conscience de la Conscience* (Delachaux et Niestle: Paris, France, 1954); *The Adolescent and His Self* (translated from the French and published by Educational Explorers Limited: Reading, England, 1962); and *For the Teaching of Mathematics* (three volumes, Educational Explorers Limited: Reading, England, 1963). He has doctorates in mathematics (from the University of Basel) and psychology (from the University of Lille).

This book was designed by Samuel N. Antupit. The text is set in Janson, a linotype face misnamed for Anton Janson, a Dutch type cutter who worked in Leipzig about 1700. The design is Dutch, however, and of that period, but the designer is unknown. Original matrices are now in the possession of the Stempel Foundry in Frankfurt. Chapter titles and other display matter are set in Normande Condensed, a face cut by the Berthold Foundry in 1931 but based upon a design from the Wilson Foundry of 1843. The book has been printed by photo-offset on Hammermill's Lockhaven Antique. Endpapers are Lindenmeyr's Multicolor.